D1826154

Imagination and the Art of the Jury Trial

Imagination and the Art of the Jury Trial

Neil Thomas

Library of Congress Control Number:		2017916872
ISBN:	Hardcover	978-1-5434-6311-8
	Softcover	978-1-5434-6312-5
	eBook	978-1-5434-6313-2

Print information available on the last page.

Rev. date: 11/20/2017

To order additional copies of this book, contact:
Xlibris
1-888-795-4274
www.Xlibris.com
Orders@Xlibris.com
766956

Contents

PART II
COMPOSITION AND PERFORMANCE

THE AUTHOR WISHES to express his deepest appreciation to Joy Baxter for her terrific contribution to the creation of this book. A recent graduate of the University of Tennessee Law School and a concert pianist, Joy brought to this book one of its foundation blocks–Schenkerian analysis–an analysis used in symphonic creation. She also introduced to the author symphonic concepts which are equally applicable to the creation of a story which is persuasive to a jury.

JOY BAXTER

Joy Baxter earned a bachelor of arts degree in music from Lipscomb University in Nashville, Tennessee. She attended L' Academie Internationale d'ete in Nice, France, where she studied piano performance with Philippe Entremont (Conductor Laureate of the Vienna Chamber Orchestra and the Israel Chamber Orchestra), Marie Joseph-Jude, and Judy Chin. Many musical traditions of excellence are passed orally from instructor to instructor. Joy's piano pedagogy lineage is only five instructors away from Beethoven and six instructors away from Mozart. She also holds a performance certificate and a music theory certificate from the Associated Board of Royal Schools of Music. She has performed at patron galas and special events at the Schermerhorn Symphony Center in Nashville, Tennessee. She obtained her law degree with advocacy emphasis at the University of Tennessee in 2017 and has joined the firm of Ortale, Kelley, Herbert & Crawford in Nashville, Tennessee.

The author also wishes to acknowledge the contributions of Kerren Berz, who provided valuable advice with respect to the symphonic concepts for this book.

Kerren Berz's talents span the musical spectrum. Currently in her 15th season as Columbus (GA) Symphony Orchestra's Concertmaster, she has also performed, recorded and toured with the Atlanta Symphony, the Harlem Festival Orchestra, and the Nashville Chamber Orchestra, whose "music without boundaries" mission produced critically acclaimed performances and recordings of music by Aaron Copeland, Conni Ellisor, and Jay Ungar, among others. In addition to the classical music field, Ms. Berz is well respected in the popular music industry.

PROLOGUE

THIS BOOK HAS been written to challenge jury trial lawyers to approach the preparation and trial of a jury case from a different point of view. Presentation of a jury case can be a form of art, and an analogous form of art can be a symphony. That analogy has been used together with an admonition to jury trial lawyers to talk and think like a normal person and use the creativity of imagination in preparing for and presenting the case. Barristers, litigators, attorneys, and shysters have tried cases for centuries, but only trial lawyers have tried jury trials. What is the point? The point is that successful trial lawyers approach the contest as an art form. In all its forms, art is an expression of emotion, of human experience. A canvas or a piece of marble is an expression of creativity either in color or stone–a human signature or a landscape as seen by its creator as perceived by the viewers. On another spectrum is the auditory expression of emotion by its creator and understood by its listener. A symphony is the expression of a series of notes received with pleasure by the listener. A jury trial is the expression told in the form of persuasion and received either with a chord struck or restruck.

In order for a jury trial to be an art form, the complete thinking taught and received in legal training must be placed in perspective. Why did I, your author, believe this book to be important? With art as our foundation and the symphony as our building, I do not intend this book to be anything more than a stimulus for thinking. If you disagree with some of the suggestions, use your own, but use your creativity, not someone else's—*yours!* Get back in touch with yourself and the world you left when you graduated from law school. You spent three years of hibernation in the study of law and left with some wonderful tools. But those tools will not build anything without a vision of what you want to build —what you want to create in the story of your trial. This book is, therefore, not intended to deal with the mechanics, per se, but rather, it deals with creativity. In being creative, you must lose rigidity. One of the main encumbrances with which we have become bound is legalese. Another encumbrance is rigid thinking. Legalese must be abandoned, and rigid thinking must give way to creativity.

Thus, there are three concepts which are central to this work, to law, and to music. One, already mentioned, is imagination (self-creativity). The second is relating (the ability to tell a story or compose a symphony and relate it to a jury). Third—and most important—is learning to overcome the biggest deficit of a lawyer and the most important attribute of a composer—listening. You have heard the words, but do you understand what was said or what just happened? In short, stop talking and start listening.

To understand what I need to try a jury trial, we must understand what we have been given to begin the process. The national trend in legal education is now geared more toward equipping students for practice rather than simply teaching principles. Law schools are using practical learning experiences, clinic, trial advocacy courses, and small groups to teach the tactics of a strong cross-examination or the essential components of a closing argument. But respectfully, these programs do not reach enough. This book attempts to expand that legal education.

Next, let us look at another vantage from which this book encourages lawyers to see their trials–interdisciplinary perspective. Put in another way, we will examine the perspective from which we look at trial advocacy. Composers use their perspective to write music for their audiences. How does he do it? How does the engineer think to create the machine? How does the doctor learn to treat the patient? The learning objective for the reader is to find analogies in these relationships that enhance one's technical knowledge of trial advocacy and collegial relationships. Use the tools given to you in law school and build on them with different ways of thinking. How would another learned discipline view this same set of facts at which you are looking?

With this challenge for you to use creativity, let me introduce some concepts which will be discussed later in more detail. By way of digression, let me say that working on this book has been fun because I have tried to stretch our imaginations in attempting to meld trial concepts with symphony concepts. My starting point is different from what has been traditionally taught to prepare a jury trial. I focus on elements of a cause of action as the foundation upon which the trial is constructed, not witnesses. Witnesses are merely the vehicle for the expression of the emotion of the elements of a cause of action. I then judge what I am creating by "tonality"–a concept discussed later in the book, which is central to judging your case. By tonality, I mean "what sounds attractive to a jury." This is similar to listening to what sounds–or can be made to sound good to a symphony audience. I believe that there is a quasi-scientific way to chart a jury's interest or disinterest, and I will show you how to do it. I will introduce you to a new way of scoring your trial. I will introduce you to macro and micro mapping–actually scoring (composing) a jury trial! I will have notes and musical instruction which can be critiqued, but I warn you, it will be different.

Other concepts which I stress are practice and self-examination. Law students attend trial practice courses. Typically, these courses consist of a lecture, followed by a small group that practices an element of the trial, under the tutelage of a practitioner. However, it is not practiced and practiced again. Imagine a young piano student who attends a performance class. He listens to the instructor describe how to play a passage, watches videos of others playing the passage, and observes a PowerPoint presentation on proper finger technique. Then this same piano student goes to a master class and is given the opportunity to play the piece two times, subject to critique by his peers. Is that student ready to take that piece to Carnegie Hall? Of course not. Neither is the law student ready for his first trial.

And that brings me to practice and introspection. Music students understand that, in order to succeed, they must practice for copious amounts of time. This book teaches law students how to think like music students, how to self-analyze and reflect upon performances to gain mastery of their art. Without practice, newly obtained trial skills are mechanical, lacking the natural informality to which juries respond so well. Law school courses are typically insular; this book seeks to be interdisciplinary.

Before ending the prologue, let me give you a word of caution. Some judges may not be receptive to the innovation I am suggesting. Before you try to use my theories, make sure your judge will let you. Also, some practitioners may resist what I espouse in this work. Both judges and practitioners are comfortable in knowing that the way we presently try cases is the "safe" way from the standpoint of appellate review. Let me urge the judicial system to at least consider what I am suggesting.

INTRODUCTION

PART OF THIS book emphasizes that a lawyer should relearn to use normal language that everyone understands. It also stresses that a jury trial needs to be tried so that a jury understands what story is being told in terms they understand. The comedy portion of that is seen in the movie *My Cousin Vinny*, and a beautiful example is as follows:

Vinny: Is it possible that the two youts?

Judge: Uh. The two what? Uh. Uh. What was that word?

Vinny: Uh. What word?

Judge: Two what?

Vinny: What?

Judge: Did you say youts?

Vinny: Yeah, two youts.

Judge: What's a yout?

Vinny: Oh, excuse me, Your Honor, two youths.

So thanks to the cast and production of *My Cousin Vinny*, and let me start with what this book is not. This book is not a book of magical secrets that lets you know how to prepare for and try every jury trial. There is no such magic. But there is art in a jury trial. Art is creativity in a symphony, in a culinary creation, in an oil on canvas, or in a sculpture. Art in a symphony is the communication of tonal and atonal sound. In a culinary creation, it is the communication of an aromatic taste; in an oil painting or sculpture, it is the communication of subtle sight and movement; and in a jury trial, it is the communication of the words and emotion of a story. All these forms of art are received *through* and *with* emotion.

Not everyone possesses the innate ability to be the best there is in a chosen medium. Beethoven had to work at it with his first try, his second try, even his third. While Mozart could intuitively create an entire symphony with the flow of the pen, so it is with trial lawyers. Some instinctively know the concepts which I will discuss; others have to work at it. So all of you, Ludwigs, start to have fun with what you are doing. That's part of the process! All I am trying to do with this book is to give you some ideas so that you can use your own powers of listening and imagination. What I want to do is provoke you to use your innate creative powers of persuasion.

Jury trials are fundamentally about common sense and everyday communication. Part of communication must be listening. When you graduated from law school, you were given a different way of thinking and talking; you were proficient in the law of evidence and civil procedure. Now you must learn how to use that law selectively and effectively to communicate with imagination and realism. You must take your legal building blocks and use description skills to relate your story. You must create an experience through the art of *imagination, communication,* and *listening.*

Trials, and particularly jury trials, are not the mechanical presentation of evidence through witnesses and documents; they should be experienced, not simply heard. In short, they should be forms of art. A jury trial is not a monotonous selection of words in much the same way that a concerto is a not just a collection of notes from reeds, strings, and percussion that's played using only one note. A concerto is a melodious experience where the sounds of the reeds and the strings blend to create music. It is a composition. Without composition, it is cacophony. Likewise, a jury trial should be an emotional experience, not just boring witness after boring witness paraded in order to make a written record. It is the weaving together of the elements of your cause of action (your story) to create an experience. A mechanical presentation of evidence is the performance of a sequence of notes that has no passion or musicality. It is simply one "middle C" after another. The "middle C" is a wonderful note by itself, but it becomes very boring when it is the only note played during the entire trial. But a variety of notes, played either fortissimo (extremely loud) or pianissimo (extremely soft), keeps the jury's attention, and they listen to your story. Much like an audience experiencing a symphony, a jury should feel the emotion of a trial.

To start the creation of a symphony or a jury trial, you have to assemble elements. The reeds, strings, percussion, and brass are the forces of the symphony. The elements of the cause of action are the jury trial equivalent to those forces. The notes and the instructions in the score by themselves are just that–notes with no emphasis and no melody. Together, they start to form something–the structure of the symphony. The elements of a cause of action (the story) become the musical structure of the trial. Either in a symphony or in a jury trial, notes and words without structure and description have no melody; they are not an experiential, emotional story.

We often reminisce about the oratory of truly great trial lawyers, but a great trial, like a great symphony, is more than oratory and Hollywood. It requires planning, strategy, and hard work. A trial lawyer combines the characteristics and talents of a writer and composer, a director, a psychologist, a head coach, and indeed, a chef. The forward to the great cookbook of the Culinary Institute of America discusses *mise en place,* a basic culinary term, meaning *to put in place* as follows:

> It means far more than simply assembling all the ingredients, pots and pans, plates, and serving pieces needed for a particular period. It is also a state of mind. Someone who has truly grasped the concept is able to keep many tasks in mind simultaneously, weighing and assigning each its proper value and priority. This assures that the chef has anticipated and prepared for every situation that could logically occur during a services period.

So it is with a jury trial, but this description of a chef deals only with the preparer. As with a good recipe, the recipient is equally important. Our recipient, the jury, is a miracle to behold; for you see, a jury is a collection of twelve ordinary people who have been summoned at random and do not know each other. They participate in a process unusual to them. And yet they reach a unanimous decision to resolve the dispute presented to them. It is your job, as their friend, to help them through this process. But to do that–for you to communicate your case to them–you must use language and concepts which they can understand. They have not been to law school; they do not think and talk like lawyers are taught to think and talk, so what they receive must be in a form they understand. Most importantly, the trial will be the first time that they have heard the story with which you have lived for a year or so. A jury, like a symphony audience, reacts to what they hear. If the jury reacts favorably to your presentation, you win; if the audience (or the critics) react favorably to the presentation of the symphony, you get raves. In either event, the result depends upon the creativity of the execution of the composition and the communication of that composition in a way in which the audience understands, feels, and appreciates. The composition is the facts of the case; how they are presented is creativity.

By starting out this book with an analogy to a symphony, I do not mean to say that it is the same kind of art form. It is not. However, like a symphony, it does have structure, and the makeup of that structure is critical. In the context of the symphony before Beethoven, structure was rigid. In similar fashion, formality in the presentation of a jury trial has tended to be formal and rigid. Today, both must be more relaxed to be understood. But both a symphony and a jury trial have a theme, the elements of the story; and both have movements, the presentation of the emotions of the story. In a jury trial, the structure may be said to consist of the natural progression of its four parts: the opening statements, the direct examination, the cross-examination, and the closing arguments. We have dealt with voir dire separately from the four because voir dire is the symphonic overture to the trial; it has bits and pieces of what is to come. But voir dire is crucially different from a symphony. The conductor does not know who is in his or her audience. The trial lawyer must know that, and voir dire is the only way he or she can know, whether his or her audience will be in tune with what he or she is about to play. Direct and cross-examination are used here instead of plaintiff's case and defendant's case because our treatment of the presentation or cross-examination of a witness does not depend upon whether it is for the plaintiff or defendant.

But back to our trial and our symphony in general. Both are creations, and those creations should be composed and performed with emotion so that they persuade or entertain. They are not just component parts but rather a sum of parts which leads to an experience. They should fit smoothly together and be something which is understood and pleasing. In a friendly discussion, would you try to persuade your neighbor of a point the same way many lawyers simply parade witnesses before a jury and use language with which a juror is not familiar? No, a jury trial is the artful persuasion of your neighbor, using neighborly language and common sense.

And that brings us to the three foundation stones which we have already mentioned and which are the bedrock of this work. They comprise creativity–listening, relating, and imagination. *Stop right here!* First, you must learn to listen! Listening is the one great deficit of all lawyers, not just trial lawyers. For some reason, lawyers love to hear themselves speak. They tend not to listen to others, but a lawyer and, more especially, a trial lawyer, must learn how to listen and hear what is being said. A good trial lawyer will listen to everything going on around her: jurors, witnesses, the judge, opposing counsel–everyone. Not only hear it but also understand it!

Likewise, relating is a touchstone. Use it. Think about it. Don't relate with technicality. Technical sense doesn't mean it can't also be common sense. Persuade yourself and persuade others.

Just as important, the power of imagination is what you use to create that story–how you make the testimony of the witnesses fit together and reinforce each other, hopefully building to a crescendo in your presentation. So let's see how we can start to breathe life into our symphonic presentation to our audience–the jury.

In part one, we will discuss the tools and concepts we will employ in going about the work of creating the composition; and in part two, we will use those tools in the composition and performance of the elements of a jury trial: voir dire, opening statement, direct examination, cross-examination, and closing argument. This is not the beginning of an old end. It is the end of a new beginning.

PART I

THE TOOLS USED FOR COMPOSITION

CHAPTER ONE

OVERVIEW

A TRIAL IS a story. How do we create, assemble, and transform the words of a story into an experience that is emotional and to which the jury can relate? In creating the masterpiece, we must first be perfectly grounded with what we spent three years of our lives in law school learning–the law. Not only did we learn the rules of evidence and procedure but also the substantive law that applies to the particular case. That knowledge must be second nature in order to be able to work the story. However, the principles of law are only the building blocks. It is the cement you create which holds the blocks together. You are providing the mortar. The law student is taught in three years what the rules are, but they are rarely taught how to use them. They may know whether they can object but not whether they should. Don't ever forget that the rules do not move the trial; the trial moves the rules.

A conservatory can teach a student the scales, but if they are played mechanically without passion, they are meaningless.

Let me be quick to point out that I do not mean to demean what has been learned in law school. I mean only to place it in its proper context. In order to try a jury trial, all the legal knowledge to be associated with that trial–both substantive and procedural–must be the firm foundation. It is only when that firm foundation exists that the lawyer can focus totally on what is going on in front of him or her. I may have a hearsay objection based on what I know of the law and the facts of this case, but do I use it? Frequent objections offend a jury, and they may think you are trying to hide something from them if you continuously object. Using a term which I will discuss later, you become *atonal*.

Let's look again at another problem that you have acquired. You have learned a new way of thinking and talking. Some call it legalese. Remember, juries have not been to law school, so don't talk with them as if they have been. Formality and stiffness needs to give way to informality–even colloquialism– but not phony colloquialism. For example, rather than starting a direct examination with "Please state your name" or even "Please introduce yourself to the jury," what about "Tell us who you are." Then "Tell us what you know about this accident." The lawyer then steps aside and lets the witness talk with the jury. Also, notice that the word *us* was used in the question rather than *the jury*. Use of the word *us* places you and the jury together. Don't become used to legal jargon. The minute you come across a justification for something based upon "that's the way it has always been done," ask the question, "Why?" Use your common sense to question constantly why you are doing something. Don't do it because that's the way it has always been done. Rather, ask if that is the way it should be done using common sense. And don't worry if your answer to the question

"Why?" is right or wrong. The critical part is that you have asked it. That brings me to the introduction of a musical term called tonality.

Tonality is a concept that was born in France, and the word is used to reference the harmonious relationships between notes. When something is "tonal," it sounds pleasant and familiar to one's ears. When something is "atonal," it means that one is repulsed by the relationships that the notes have with one another. To help understand some of the musical concepts I discussed, I have included with this book a list which has excerpts from compositions. Please listen to these excerpts. I hope this helps you better understand the concept I am trying to import from the musical field to the jury trial field. Track 3 on the list offers a sampling of Mozart's piano sonata. To our Western ears, that music would be considered tonal. Track 4, on the other hand, is a modern classical piece called "Black Angels," written by George Crumb. Although "Black Angels" has important significance in the modern classical music repertoire, the average listener would find it to be atonal. You might notice the music that is familiar to our ears is typically described as tonal, while the unfamiliar music is atonal. Atonality is an absolute, regardless of who is listening. The average listener may find it unpleasant or disconcerting.

It's important to recognize that tonality can be achieved from atonality through a process of repetitious exposure. If you hate modern classical music, try listening to it for a solid month. By the end of the second week, you will begin to hear tonality within the atonality. Your ear will adjust and make sense of the sounds to which you are continuously being exposed. There are some attorneys that are so aggressive that juries hate them, unless the trial lasts longer than three days. After three days, the jury may begin to realize that the aggressive attorney is just being himself, and they become more accustomed to him.

Suddenly, they decide that they like him. What happened? The attorney's atonality became tonal to the jury. They were exposed to the attorney for an extended time, and some of the things the attorney said rang true. The attorney became familiar. Remember atonality becomes tonality only if repeated over time. Learn to recognize whether you or your story are atonal and see if you can get rid of the atonality.

Something is either tonal or atonal. The use of this term does not mean that a trial lawyer who doesn't hear the difference can't be a good trial lawyer. It just means that he could not compose a symphony. Tonal and atonal in the context of a jury trial focuses on attraction and repulsion which, as I have said, are the synonyms for the two terms. This process is all about knowing your jury, which requires that you discover what they consider to be tonal or atonal. Stravinsky's ballet masterpiece, *The Rite of Spring,* caused fistfights to break out in the Champs Elysees Theater when it premiered in May 1913. The ballet dancers, instead of twirling on tiptoes, were thumping and jumping. The music was fierce, raw, and aggressive. The audience was hissing and booing the first few notes. Hell broke loose not long after. As music has evolved and our notions of tonality have expanded, Stravinsky's piece is considered to be one of the greatest classical music pieces of his time. Rock bands such as Kiss and film and symphony composers like John Williams have all borrowed phrases and concepts from Stravinsky's work to create some of the best beloved music. At the time *The Rite of Spring* premiered, it was far ahead of its time to be well received.

There are many lawyers who find themselves in disfavor with a jury because they have failed to evaluate the response that they will likely receive. Some attorneys may be ahead of their time. Either way, it is a loss. To be a successful trial attorney, you have to learn to chart a jury's tonality. In the context which I have just described, the tonality of a jury may depend on the juror's age (mood and tonality change from generation to generation), cultural background, or community involvement. Tonality can become synonymous with stereotyping. The use of the term *stereotyping* is not being used in a derogatory sense. It is being used to ascertain what appeals to a type of person—what is his or her tone—and honing in on that appeal. One cannot persuade unless one knows what persuades. This concept will have significant impact upon the discussion of voir dire. In that process, I am not just eliminating jurors who may not be favorable to my story but learning what appeals to the jurors and using that appeal to my advantage.

Imagine a spectrum of tonality that looks like this:

ATONAL (unfamiliar)   TONAL (familiar)

Black Angels (Track 4)   Perle Etudes (Track 5)   Stravinsky (Track 6)   Wagner (Track 7)   Mozart (Track 8)

Notice that the chart is arranged with the least pleasant piece—I am presuming that my average reader is not a twenty-first-century classical music fan—to the most pleasant-sounding piece. This is my spectrum of tonality. Every juror has a similar spectrum. Here's a sample juror tonality spectrum:

ATONAL (unfamiliar)   TONAL

Memories of past abuse   Trips to the Dentist   Sitting in traffic   Having dinner with family   Winning the lottery

Also, don't ever forget that a jury trial is not about trying to impress the jury with how much you know. You are a persuader, not a debater. A jury trial is not point and counterpoint; it is all about persuasion. You may think at this point that a story is just for the plaintiff to tell, and that it is up to the defendant to "rebut" that story. Nothing could be further from the truth. Remember the old phrase: "There are two sides to every argument." If there are two sides, then there are two stories. Sure each side must "deal with" the other side's story, but each side must have its own. So tell your own story. And if you don't have one to tell, do one of two things–settle or admit what you have to and defend what you can. If you don't have a responsive story, you are better off in front of the jury "fessing up" that on this point, the other side is right and defend your strong point. That gives you credibility with the jury. If you are the defendant and if liability is clear, admit it and go after the plaintiff's damages. Even if you are defending damages only, concede the damages which are clear. You will be starting to analyze and organize your case along new lines, the elements of your cause of action or defense.

What other general suggestions do we have? Note, I would refer to *suggestions* because I want to avoid using the term *rules*. Rules should be used only when you know why you are using these rules. Always ask the question "Why?" If you can't answer the question, don't use the rule.

Let me go back to the basic three suggestions which permeate this book and which are common both to symphonies and to jury trials–imagining, listening, and relating–all of which are part of common sense. However, the most important is listening. As I say, over and over again, by his or her very nature and three years of training, a trial lawyer does not make a good listener. To be a good trial lawyer, you must listen. If you don't learn to listen, every case you try, you will lose. When you listen, listen with your mind, not just your ears. Think about what is being heard. What did you hear? What are you being told?

The Use of Imagination

In using your *imagination,* approach the trial and its fact pattern from the vantage of the big picture. What is the dispute between the parties? What is each complaining the other did or did not do? What is the context in which they did it or did not do it? Don't focus at first on the details of the dispute. Look at the overall controversy. Look at the big picture. What happened that created this dispute? Why did it happen? How did it happen? What was the environment in which it happened? These are just the starting points.

Take, for example, a lawsuit between two large airplane manufacturers. One (the sub) was making sections of the plane for the other. When the sub started shipping those sections to the other, all kinds of defects showed up. The sub said that the defects were the result of inadequate plans given by the other. Looking at the hundreds of defects being experienced, it looks like the sub might be right. But when the main manufacturer put all the defects into a computer and looked at the "big picture," it clearly showed that all the defects were related to each other and were the result of the sub's poor manufacturing processes. The defendant looked at the big picture of the entire process, not just the individual defects. Case over.

The big picture is not limited to lawsuits. It can be used in administrative rulemaking. In the not-too-distant past, the Environmental Protection Agency issued rules on the amount of mercury which could be present in water discharged from manufacturing plants. One manufacturer was particularly hit hard by the low levels proposed and contested the regulation. The manufacturer believed that there was no scientific studies to show a health hazard in levels of mercury that low. If that was going to be the battle line to draw with the EPA, the manufacturer was going to lose. The EPA could always find an epidemiological study to justify the regulation level under judicial scrutiny. Rather, in the administrative proceedings, the proposed level was attacked because the manufacturer showed that there was no enforcement instrumentation sensitive enough to detect the proposed levels with accurate enough results to support enforcement. The EPA backed off because the level itself was not attacked, but the inability to enforce the level was.

How is imagination used in a symphony, and how can it be used in the same way in a jury trial? A symphonic example is "Peter and the Wolf." In that piece, certain instruments are used to depict certain characters, whether it is Peter, the wolf, or the grandfather. Whenever the listener hears that instrument, there is an immediate association with that character. In a jury trial, those associations can also be used, whether by physical description, clothing, or facial expression. In a robbery case, a lawyer wanted to plant the idea of what $100,000 looked like, so he showed the jury $100,000 in a briefcase (using only $100 bills on top of stocks of paper bills). Throughout the trial, when he referred to the defendant, he placed his hand on the briefcase that sat on his counsel table just beside the jury. By the end of the trial, when the attorney mentioned the defendant, the eyes of the jury would automatically glance toward the briefcase. What began as a physical association (placing his hand on the briefcase when discussing the defendant) ended as a mental association.

How about imagination in creating the story? If you don't have a story to tell, don't go to trial. When preparing your story, think of the following questions:

As a matter of law, what do I have to prove? What do I want to tell the jury? How do I want to tell it? What is going to have the most impact? How will I make sure it has the most impact? Does it make sense? Use your imagination, creativity and thought in coming up with your game plan. Where am I going, and how am I going to get there? Sometimes you can use your imagination and your opponent to "get there." For example, a horrendous car accident–a van was squashed into a crane by a pickup truck on the highway straightaway, on a clear day at noon with no traffic. It was difficult to understand why the defendant had not seen the plaintiff–other than through absolute inattention. Plaintiff's counsel used imagination when he took the defendant driver's deposition. Rather than starting off with an hour of boring background details, he asked the person's name followed by "How far away were you when you first saw Mr. Jones's van?" The resulting answer was the most candid, accurate answer about the young man's version of the accident that the plaintiff's lawyer could have gotten. He was, by his testimony, only one hundred feet away from the point of impact. And all because the plaintiff's lawyer didn't play by the rules and used his imagination to surprise a witness into a candid answer for which he was not prepared.

Relating Your Story

After creating your story with imagination, *relate* your story. Relating is nothing more than taking a complex set of facts and reducing them to something simple, which people can understand or relate to. In a securities case, relating meant not arguing whether one geological drill core was assayed at a certain percentage of silver so as to constitute material inside information. Rather, it was argued that this find was significant enough that the directors bought the stock of the company. Relating means explaining in simple terms what happened. You have lived with this case for as much as three or more years, and you know it backward and forward. You have to simplify what you have learned over that period of time so that the jury understands it. Practice telling your story to someone who doesn't know anything about the case, and see what he or she understands and doesn't understand.

Listening

Finally–and more important than imagination or relating–is *listening*. It is amazing what you can hear if you just listen. Listen to what the witness is telling you in depositions or the way the witness is telling it at trial. The way that something is said may be just as important as what is being said. Don't listen to what you are saying; listen to what the others are saying. Listening may result in a spontaneous addition to the story. An example of listening during the trial occurred as late as the defendant's closing argument. The plaintiff's story involved the defendant cleaning out his tanker trucks and directing the oily refuse through a hose onto the plaintiff's land. The defendant admitted to the wrongdoing but said that because the land was in the flood plain, the plaintiff simply wasn't damaged. Rather than go through example after example of what the plaintiff could not use his land for, the defendant argued that the plaintiff's property was flood plain property. In support of that story and in closing, counsel meant to say that the plaintiff's damages were not significant enough and that the jury should not award significant damages. Unfortunately, his choice of words was that this whole thing was "no big deal." Plaintiff's counsel heard what he said and responded by looking at the jury, without saying a word, and then repeated with a question mark, "No big deal?" He continued, "It may be no big deal to a Minnesota trucking company, but here in the South, a man's land is a big deal." The jury awarded not only compensatory damages but also punitive damages. The plaintiff's attorney was listening.

Another example of listening occurred in a simple car wreck. In this case, the defendant's theme was that the wreck was a simple tap and that the plaintiff had exaggerated her damages. The evidence showed this through the photographs of the two cars. The defendant admitted negligence but contested the plaintiff's damages. Rather than focus on the absence of damage, the plaintiff said that the case was all about "taking responsibility" because the defendant could not explain the accident (because she could not remember the accident). Not a bad approach to a case with no visible damage to the plaintiff's car. Complaining that the defendant had refused to take responsibility for the accident, the plaintiff's attorney closed with an example. He told the jury that if his son had hit a ball through a neighbor's window and had confessed his error to him, he would have been proud, gone to the neighbor, and offered to pay for the window. After having listened to the plaintiff's argument, defense counsel then rose and said that if his son had done the same thing, he too would have been proud and would have gone to the neighbor and offered to pay. The defense counsel then added that his neighbor was different from the plaintiff's neighbor because his neighbor not only wanted the broken window fixed but also the kitchen redecorated.

Once you have the story, never lose sight of that story no matter how detailed the trial becomes. The people in that jury box have been brought in off the street. They don't know each other and don't have the slightest idea about all the complexities of a jury trial, even though they are at the center of it. Keep it simple. Keep it on track. Keep your ears open.

When you tell the story with your evidence, use only the evidence that has a place in the story. If a piece of evidence doesn't have a place and fits in with the story line, the jury will become confused and wonder why they heard it. They will get sidetracked. All parts of the case should have something in it to remind the jury of the story. Whether the part is the opening, direct examination, cross-examination, or closing, it should have some reference to the story that reinforces the story. One final comment about your story. Get the story in your mind. Get all the details of the story in your mind. During your preparation of the case, if you hear something that doesn't fit with the picture of the story you have in your mind, ask yourself, "Why?" Either something is wrong with the story or something is wrong with what you just heard. Figure out why. Listen logically to see if something has a place.

Schenkerian Analysis and the Elements

I have covered some of the rudimentary concepts which many trial lawyers have already used in a trial with a jury. This territory I want to cover now is new. What I am going to suggest is a way of composing your jury trial, which is different from the way in which most trial lawyers have been accustomed to preparing it. Although the discussion will be divided into the traditional components of a trial–voir dire, opening, direct, cross, and closing–I will approach each from a different vantage point–the vantage point of the composition and performance of a symphony. Although the structure of the jury trial will remain the same, its method of creation will differ. Although your story will be the cohesive force–the mortar which will hold your building blocks together–the methodology of its creation will borrow more from symphonic concepts. I will start with the building blocks–the elements of your cause of action (our legal terminology for your story). I will then order those elements in terms of the emotional impact of each on your audience–the jury–in much the same way as the movements of a symphony are ordered for their emotional impact upon the audience. I will then build those elements with our cement–lay testimony, exhibits, expert testimony, and visual aids. That cement will be our strings, brass, woodwinds, and tympani, but my elements are the foundation and focus.

To do all this, however, let me introduce you to Schenkerian analysis.

Heinrich Schenker (1868–1935) was a German musician and music theorist. He invented what is now known as Schenkerian analysis, a method of cataloging or isolating basic notes within a single passage or within an entire piece. His analysis is critical to approach, but I am actually going to reverse his process in order to create the composition for our jury trial.

What did Schenker do in analyzing a symphony? He started with complex, frilly passages and reduced them to your basic elements. Take a look at this example:

In the example above, the first and topmost line is the original passage from the piece in its final form. It is somewhat complex and interrelated. The line below the first is a reduction or a simplification of the first line. Schenker reduced the complex chords, runs, trills, and combinations of notes to the recurrent notes–those notes which were the basic building blocks of the symphony. Finally, he ended up with one or two essential notes that he perceived to be the base of the entire passage. That last simplified line (known as the Ursatz) reveals the most important, fundamental notes of the piece. Listen to track 1 on the list found in the back of the book.

What I suggest is in order to create your jury trial, you reverse Schenkerian' analysis to build your composition. Build your case by starting with the elements of your cause of action, the essential notes. Examine each for its contributory impact to your whole case. Which element packs the most emotion? Which has the least? Which will become the most important block? Place your emphasis on building that block or blocks. This concept applies to the defendant as well. Which are the most important blocks in your defense? Are these blocks plaintiff's weakest? Along the same lines, which of your affirmative defenses are the most important?

Instead of recurrent and fundamental notes to build our symphony, I will use the elements of the cause of action or defense as our fundamental notes. I will perform this construction not only for each individual element of your story (your cause of action) but also in combining these elements to build the ultimate, finished composition for your symphonic story. In jury trials, I have become accustomed to building the trial around the witnesses called the ordering of the witnesses. In the Schenkerian approach, I build the story around its elements. The witnesses, exhibits, and visual aids are the runs, trills, and chords. The elements, in turn, combine to become the movements of the symphony which are then presented to give each element its maximum impact. Thus, the element–whether it be duty, breach of duty, causation, or damage–becomes the primary emotional driver, with the witness (or the other supporting instruments) as the secondary driver. This enhances the emotional impact of the primary driver. All this culminates in the repetition of the elements used by you in your direct and cross-examination, closing argument, and finally, by the judge in his charge. This culminating connection to the charge does not usually occur in the traditional method of trying a case.

Let me be quick to point out that some lawyers who possess the innate ability to try jury trials do what I have been describing without thinking. They are the Mozarts. The rest of us are the

Beethovens who must chart it out, scratch it out, and rechart it. At this point, I want to give a small illustration of this process, but the elaboration of the concept will be dealt with in more detail in the individual chapters to follow.

Let's approach a trial by separating and examining the elements, whether tort, contract, or anything else. A tort cause of action is divided into four basic elements: duty, breach of duty, causation, and damages. Depending upon the nature of a particular case, one element will be more important than the others. Let's take a bad car wreck. For the plaintiff, the breach and the damages will probably be the most emotional issues, while duty and causation will be the lesser. (Causation will often be a defense emphasis.) The importance of each will depend upon the facts of each particular case. In presenting the case to the jury, I will spend most of my effort on those two elements, although all must be proved. I may simply want to use one or two witnesses or exhibits on the lesser elements while concentrating our visual aids, exhibits, demonstrative videos, reenactments, and indeed, music (if the plaintiff cannot now hear) in support of the other elements. I may want to use three supportive devices on breach and five on damages. But what I have done for each element is to assign single notes to the lesser important, chords to the more important, and runs and trills to the most important, together with the judge's instruction which goes with it. From a defense standpoint, the main element may be the defense of a preexisting condition to show that the plaintiff's condition was not caused by the accident.

What is being described so far may be called a macro plan (a plan for the relationship among the elements). The next step is to place in order the presentation of the elements. This decision is a judgment call but will depend upon the use of your imagination and common sense as to what will have the most emotional impact and where. For each witness a micro plan is prepared. The micro plan for a witness for an unimportant element may simply be the script. For a more important element, the micro plan will be the script combined with the visual and auditory aids you will use with that witness.

You will want to be careful not to create a great deal of boring, stuffy knowledge. Can repetitious, boring information be interesting? Yes, actually, it can. The second movement of Beethoven's "Symphony No. 7" takes the musical form of a chaconne. The first sound you hear is a chordal progression, a simple rhythm, and some dark chords. Those same chords are repeated throughout the entire piece, but the effect is far from boring. (Listen to track 2 on your list.) That is because they are different. Are the parts of your elements interestingly different or boringly the same?

Beethoven adds color after color atop the chordal progression so that your ear perceives a different sound every time. You are, in fact, hearing the same chords every time. Say aloud, "You do not have to restate my theme verbatim continuously throughout the trial. I can get my point across by using different words each time. Or I can use the same words but surround them in different contexts so that they feel more natural. Thus, they are not boring. They are engaging." *Repeat!*

One final point in my Schenkerian analysis borrows from psychology and from the symphony. How does the witness look and act while testifying? How does the lawyer look and act while questioning? Use your video camera to analyze and critique both. Both should know how they look and sound prior to appearing before the jury. Can any changes be made? Are the two compatible, or do you want to change the examiner or cross-examiner (more difficult) before the jury? Do you want Matlock or Raymond Burr?

There is one more musical concept which I want to introduce to round out my preliminary discussion before I go into the different phases of the trial. That is counterpoint, sometimes called contrapuntal analysis. Counterpoint is the art of setting one musical line against another, according to the rules that assist the composer in creating tonality. The goal of the study of counterpoint, as one author puts it, is to "awaken or sharpen in students a feeling for the contrapuntal element that is present to some degree in virtually all music; to make them sensitive to the forces of opposition and agreement, tension and relaxation, direction, climax, and the like that operate when two or more separate voices are sounded simultaneously." In other words, when two or more separate melodies are playing at the same time, these melodies can be manipulated to create tonality—the notion that composers refer to as contrapuntal harmony or counterpoint. This concept has an application to the jury trial because it helps create the tonality we desire to achieve. Counterpoint is not used to enhance our own melody, but it is used to make the opponent's tonality your tonality. It is the adaptation of your opponent's element with your opponent's tonality and making it tonal to your position.

Before the student composer can join two individual melodies together to create contrapuntal harmony, he or she has to be assured that the lines are independently good. Before the lawyer can create tonality for the jury, he or she must be certain that his or her "melody" will provide the appropriate counterpoint to his opponent's melody. There must be balance.

So what are the fundamental building blocks of a good melody? Or for your purposes, what creates a good story? First, there must be a good sense of direction that the ear or mind perceives, leading to a climax. This creates what composers call melodic contour or what an author would refer to as a pleasing storyline or plot.

After you are certain that your melody, your story, has independent value, you start to listen to your opponent's melody (his primary elements) so that you can combine the two in a way that benefits you. Here are some fundamental principles of two-voice counterpoint taken from Prof. Kenty Kennan's handbook on counterpoint:

1. Each line must be good in itself.
2. There must be sufficient independence between the voices in terms of direction and rhythmic motion.
3. On the other hand, they must have enough in common, stylistically and otherwise, so that they will fuse into a convincing whole when combined.
4. The lines must imply a good harmonic suggestion. At any given point, the ear hears not only the horizontal lines but also the vertical result of combining them; these vertical sounds must represent a satisfactory harmonic progression.

Now let's apply these principles to our case. First, you have control over only your story line, not your opponent's but you know how to attack it. Then there must be independence between the two stories (elements), but this is simply opposition. Step three is more problematic. A jury generally does not pick one story presented to it over another, although their verdict does. Rather, the jury is trying to figure out "what's going on" as a combination of two stories. Your story or presentation of your strong element has to be more reasonable than the other side's position on that element or elements. The fourth step is to have behind your element a public policy or justice foundation. Finally, you come back to step three and see whose element or story fits best into the big picture.

What you now have done is to create a trial script–a macro script–which can actually be viewed; its presentation and melody will appear on a page and can be critiqued from a new vantage point. Traditionally, most trial lawyers will script the testimony for each witness (micro scripts) without seeing how those scripts may fit together or how they may "sound" when visually experienced. Each individual micro script may also be seen from the standpoint of variations in tone and emphasis. This results in the macro view of the trial as a whole and a micro view of the testimony of each witness. The result is that the story is presented with power and emotion.

CHAPTER TWO

THE EMPEROR AS A CLIENT

T HE POPULAR FILM *Amadeus* depicts the meeting of Wolfgang Amadeus Mozart and Joseph II, the Holy Roman Emperor of the Habsburg lands. The relationship between them was a delightful one. Mozart composed masterpieces for the emperor, while the emperor looked on and gave light instructions. Joseph II was a sophisticated client who had a general working knowledge of music, but it was Mozart who retained full autonomy over the construction of the pieces. Like the composer and the commissioner, the attorney and his client retain interesting boundaries. The client pays the bill and wants a specific outcome, while the lawyer controls the composition and presentation of the case.

I don't want to dwell at length on this subject because it could take up a whole book by itself with the intricacies of the psychology of the attorney-client relationship. I touch on it because I believe the client must be involved with the planning and must understand the general nature of the planning. The client can also provide critical advice, especially in terms of facts, which he or she may not have told you but get triggered by his or her recollection. Remember that this is the beginning of a special relationship. Although this relationship is a close one, you must never ever lose your objectivity. Your client depends on it, and the trial depends upon it. You don't have to distrust what your client says, but you must always ask yourself, "Does this make sense?" Because if it doesn't make sense to you, you can rest assured that the jury won't think it makes sense either.

So make sure the client understands that when you press him or her about the facts they are telling you, it's not that you don't trust them; it's just that you need to make sure you have identified any weaknesses that there may be in the case. Remember, they come to you with "their story" already in their mind, but it is naturally from their perspective. So ask yourself, "What has been overlooked? What have we missed? How have I misperceived it?" If you haven't overlooked anything and the case still doesn't look good, don't be afraid to advise the client to try to settle or not bring suit at all. Disregard your client's assertion that Aunt Minnie's best friend in Iowa got $100,000 for a similar case. This case is in your town with your jurors. Be able to tell the client what jury verdicts in cases have been. You are there to evaluate and advise. Lawyers are attorneys, but they are also "counselors at law." Present the settlement option with objectivity in terms both of what the case looks like and what the case is going to cost.

Next, make sure that you keep the client involved so that the client knows all developments. At the outset, explain the process and how tough it is going to get. Prepare the client for having their credibility and background brought out. On that point, you have got to get the client to disclose the "skeletons in the closet." Keep your client involved with everything happening in the case. They may see something you have missed. In a leaking shingle case—I will later discuss—it was the client who came up with a fact which was absolutely critical to the case. He knew more about the construction project than the lawyer did. But don't let them take over in strategizing the case. You need to be firm but open to suggestion. Don't let the client control the boat. If it gets down to a fundamental disagreement over strategy, put your foot down. Don't ever be too proud to say, "I think you need a new lawyer."

You also need to make yourself as tonal as possible to the client. If you want to have a good relationship, you need to fall as much within their spectrum of tonality as you can. Do not presume that the client will find you as charming as you believe you are. Be humble enough to learn what your client needs in a lawyer.

Finally, evaluate how your client will appear to and be heard by the jury. You may want to change the appearance of your client for the trial, but don't make it phony. Witnesses, photographs, or videos may show that what the jury sees is not the real person, and that is dangerous. If your client's voice is atonal because of a speech defect or physical ailment, be sure to alert the jury to that in voir dire. That was done in a case with a client who would have been heard as a gruff person, but warning of that problem in voir dire changed him into your nicest uncle. What may have been atonal has been turned into tonal. Now once you have met with the client, prepared, and filed the complaint, it's time for discovery.

CHAPTER THREE

DISCOVERY

WITH THE ADVENT of discovery, first in the federal process and then in the states, the concept of trial by ambush was abolished. But it also brought in the huge escalation of the cost of a jury trial. With the societal evolution of technology with its e-mails, text messages, cell phones, and the like, discovery has expanded even more exponentially.

Although the trial lawyer is provided with a number of tools—interrogatories, production of documents, depositions, physical and mental examinations, and the like—don't use them all. Knee-jerk discovery is not useful. Use only the tools that you actually need. This discussion will focus on the deposition.

Almost every lawyer knows how to take a deposition, but let's look at why you do it and, to a certain extent, how you do it. Here, I may depart somewhat from my symphony model, but don't forget that rehearsals for a symphony orchestra eliminate mistakes, which would occur in the performance. More importantly, the orchestra becomes accustomed to the conductor, and this is extremely important.

Obviously, you take depositions to find out what the witness knows about the facts in the case and to lock that witness in to that testimony. But how you approach the deposition depends upon whether you are taking the deposition for discovery or for later use at trial when you present your case. This distinction is important because we have seen attorneys call the opposing party at trial as a witness on their case to get facts from them that they really only need for the record to make their case. In those situations, it is much better to read those answers from a deposition rather than give your adversary the benefit of being able, permissibly, to lead his client on cross-examination after your limited questions on direct. An argument can be made that if you call your adverse party as a witness, you can get a dramatic admission. But assuming the jury even understands what you have done, it really is often much more dramatic to obtain the admission on cross-examination. So make sure in the deposition of an adverse party you nail down the answers you want to read later (or show, in the case of a video deposition) at trial instead of calling the party.

But there is another very important reason for a deposition— to see the demeanor of the witness. How does the witness look and act while testifying? It is also important depending upon your judge's charge on witness demeanor. As you will see, planning the cross-examination is not only for its content but also for its tonality or, rather, its atonality. You will need to exploit this. If the witness hurts you with the substance of his or her testimony, he or she may actually help you with the atonality of his or her testimony. The witness simply may not be a likeable witness. Rather than trying to discredit the credibility of his or her testimony, you may want to enhance the atonality of his or her testimony by getting him or her to be even more atonal. You cannot accomplish this objective, however, with a transcript of a deposition, which you can neither hear nor see. You will need a video of the deposition because the opposing lawyer may realize that the witness is atonal during his deposition (if he has not prepared him or her the way you have) and prep him or her for his or her live testimony to reduce the atonality. You will then need to show the jury that what they have seen at trial is not the real witness–the witness that was seen in the deposition. This was devastating in a death case in which a mother was asking for consortium damages for the loss of her child. In her deposition, which the jury was shown often, she was not the sympathetic mother who appeared on the stand. So if you have planned for the cross-examination of a witness who has appeared atonal in the deposition but whose tonality has changed, you will need the video.

Now how do you prepare your client mentally for the deposition? Physically, the client should be prepared for the deposition as if the deposition testimony were the trial testimony, even though it is being taken by the opposite side. There are five general suggestions. You must develop your own for the needs of your case. First, tell the truth. Abraham Lincoln has a saying, "No man has a good enough memory to be a successful liar." How true. Second, tell the client to listen to the question and every word in it. Often a questioner will emphasize certain words and not others so that the witness may miss or not focus on the undertone words. The transcript makes no such distinction (but the video will). So again, listen. Third, wait before answering, and then answer only the question. The client should wait because this gives time to object if there is an objection to the question and makes the client think about the question. The witness should be told that the transcript will not show how long it takes to answer the question. Unless the opposing attorney may make a statement on the record like, "Let the record reflect the witness took three minutes to answer the question," or the deposition is videotaped. Unfortunately, if the deposition is a video, you are stuck with it. Next, the answer should be short and sweet and be responsive to the question. The deposition is not the time to educate the other side about what the witness knows. Make the other side work for the information. That's what they are being paid to do. At the same time, don't let the witness appear obstinate or evasive if the deposition is being videotaped. Don't volunteer information even if the questioner gets a puzzled look on his face after the client answers the question. If the questioner is confused about the answer, though, that's his or her problem. A number of witnesses will feel compelled to clear up the confusion that they think they have caused. Tell them to resist that urge. Last, the client is never ever off the record, even if the court reporter stops taking down the testimony and somebody has said, "Let's go off the record." If you say something off the record that the other side can use to your disadvantage, the next thing you will see is that statement in black and white or on video on the record. A prime example of that occurred during the deposition of an engineer in the airframe subcontract case we have discussed. The defendant asserted that the problems being encountered by the plaintiff on the assembly line were being caused by poor workmanship, not the drawings supplied by the defendant. In a deposition, the plaintiff's engineer was asked whether the particular problem being discussed could have been caused by poor workmanship. The lawyer defending the witness instructed the witness not to answer because the question was a hypothetical question. The questioner asked to go off the record to explain that the question was not hypothetical but was based upon a major inspection document called a material review record. This record identified the problem as having been caused by "workmanship" because that was the block checked as being the cause of the problem. As the lawyers talked, the witness interjected, again, off the record, and said, "Oh, you know the story behind that, don't you?" to which the questioner said, "No, I don't. Tell me." The witness then blurted out that the workmanship block had been checked because if any other box had been checked, it would have shut the assembly line down. This production line was for a fighter aircraft, so the witness was asked (again off the record) whether this document was, therefore, a falsified government record, since it was delivered with the plane to the Navy, Marines, and Air Force. The witness shrugged and said, "I guess so," whereupon the questioner said, "Let's go back on the record." Unbelievably at that point, the witness's lawyer asked the witness if he had personal knowledge of what he had said, and he said, "Yes." The case was settled shortly thereafter. Off the record? Hardly.

So much for the general rules. After you have gotten the witness thoroughly frustrated with these rules, tell him that you expect all of them to be broken in the first thirty minutes of the deposition, except the last one.

Now step back and see if you are going to need to change the tonality of your client or witness. Remember, if the deposition is videoed, the appearance and demeanor of the witness is just as important as the facts testified to. It may be useful to actually video the witness yourself before the deposition so that the witness can see how he or she looks while testifying. This should also be done for trial preparation.

Clients and witnesses have often asked, "How long will this deposition take?" It is important to get an agreement or establish up front that a deposition will last no longer than four or five hours, two or three in the morning, and two or three in the afternoon. Any longer and the witness will get tired, and tired witnesses make mistakes. Also, make sure the client knows they can take breaks when they want, but there should be no discussion with the client during breaks regarding their testimony other than to say they are doing fine. Remember, a deposition is not only mental; it is also physical; and the witness, like any good musician, may become tired and do something atonal.

When taking the deposition of the opposite party, start with the knowledge that the deposition will be on his or her friendly turf–his attorney's conference room. The witness will start off with some comfort. Don't disturb that comfort, even though his attorney has told the client that you are the enemy. Be Columbo–the "shucks, I don't understand" approach. Or I am just trying to find out what you know about this case. Remember, you are trying to get as much information as you can from the person, so you want to be their friend. You get more bees with honey than with vinegar. With confrontation, the witness will clam up.

When you start the deposition, explain to the witness that you are simply trying to find out what he knows about the case, that you are not trying to trip her up and that if the witness does not understand the question, he or she should ask for it to be rephrased or restated. What you are trying to do with this up-front explanation is to keep the witness locked in to an answer and not be able to change by saying that he or she did not understand the question at the time of the deposition.

Next, when taking the deposition–as with everything else that you do as a trial lawyer–listen to what is being said. Not only listen to it but also hear it. There is a difference between listening and hearing. You listen to what is said, but you need to understand what is heard. What did that witness say in the last answer? What did he really say? Witnesses want to make sure you understand them, so they will do anything to try to clear up any confusion on your part. (Remember this from the other side.) So listen to that witness carefully and ask your next question based on that answer–not the next question on your list of questions. Once you have exhausted the line of questions precipitated by a certain answer, then you can go back to your list of questions. In that regard, never go into a deposition without any idea of where you are going. Sure, you are trying to find out the witness knows, but you are also trying to establish what they don't know or what they didn't do. What a witness did not do may be as important as what the witness did do.

There is a humorous rule about depositions. When reading them to the jury, don't do it after lunch. They can be so boring that a jury will nod off and go to sleep. Since the judge may also be asleep, he or she won't be any help. Believe it or not, the same can be true of a videotaped deposition. Although a video deposition is like watching TV, it is not the same if the lawyer fumbles with paper for two or three minutes between every question and answer. This is deadly. Go into a video deposition just as if it were the trial. With a typed transcript, the deposition may be approached in the same way that a rehearsal is approached. If it is videotaped, it is more like the production number. Be absolutely prepared. Often, if the video deposition is of an expert witness, a discovery deposition will already have been taken, so your probing should be over. Go to the heart of your examination succinctly and finish it.

Discovery is over, and the trial date looms. It is often said that the two worst times in the day of a trial lawyer are the fifteen minutes before the trial starts and the hours when the jury deliberates. During those fifteen minutes prior to trial, you worry about whether you have done everything you could to get ready. During deliberation, you realize there is nothing more you can do. It's out of your hands. So try to get rid of both of those periods of stress by being prepared. Remember Murphy's Law: if something can go wrong, it will. You are trying to keep those times when it does go wrong to a minimum. At the end of the trial, when the jury goes out to deliberate, you should feel that you did everything you could to prepare, and you tried it accordingly.

After discovery and before trial, get out of the office and away from the case. Actually, if you can do it, do this often in the preparation phase. Go to a place where you can be relaxed and think about the case and its big picture. You may even want to listen to some classical music. It really can be calming. In law school, I often went to a movie the night before exams to aid in relaxation. The best preparation does not come hurried or crammed the night before trial. It comes with a well-appointed schedule in the weeks prior.

CHAPTER FOUR

TRIAL PREPARATION

Technology

BEFORE I START looking in more detail at the elements of your cause of action and how they fit together, let's look at technology–the sections of the orchestra. Your witness is the soprano or the baritone. The audio-visual support is your string section. The elmo is your bass. Your demonstrative exhibits are your reeds. The lawyer can be the brass. You will use most of them on your major elements, which you have orchestrated on your macro. Your minor elements will receive few, if any. Your technology has become indispensable. It presents your elements in the same manner in which the jury is used to receiving other everyday information. Stories were originally repeated by word of mouth through the storyteller. They were then written and printed. At the turn of the century, they were displayed in theaters in the form of movies. Then in the

1950s, those stories came into the home with the advent of television. Now those stories are on iPads, smartphones, and desktop computers. Receipt of information and stories has been becoming increasingly visual and auditory. That trend must be utilized. The rendition of the important elements of the macro plan of your story to a jury must become increasingly visual and auditory, although it does not necessarily have to be in the form of entertainment. The presentation can be as simple as displaying a document on a screen with the use of an elmo, but use it to intensify the elements through both audio and visual techniques.

What I want to do is use technology as part of my symphony. Strings, brass, and woodwinds create a pleasing, emotional experience. Witnesses, exhibits, and video, when carefully planned, create a convincing emotional story. Lawyers can, if not carefully self-critiqued, become blaring brass or, if self-critiqued, a pleasing French horn. Without the planning, they are a cacophonous din. I have already introduced you to elemental enhancement–the support of witnesses with audio and visual aides to provide sensation to the elements of your cause of action, your story.

Before I go into high tech–because I know you have already focused on computers–let's just talk about some simple technology through the use of a courtroom clock and something as rudimentary as mathematics. Mathematics can change the facts of a case if you use your imagination. You can't change the facts, but you can change how the facts are perceived. Enter imagination. The "facts" of the case are this. Four young girls in a car are coming out of the end of a dark tunnel. They are approaching a red light where a car is stopped at the light, and they rear-end the stopped car. The driver testifies that she was paying attention, was only doing thirty miles an hour (the speed limit), and that although she saw the car in front of her, she didn't have time to react. Sounds like a pretty good defense. But on cross, you need to develop one more fact–the distance from the end of the tunnel to the red light. The driver testified on cross that it was no more than one hundred yards. Still sounds OK. Enter mathematics. Ask the witness to agree that there are 5,280 feet in a mile, which she will do. Then ask her to multiply that by thirty miles per hour, which means she was going 158,400 feet per hour. Then ask her to divide that by sixty minutes in an hour and sixty seconds in a minute, and she will undoubtedly tell you that she was going forty-four feet per second. Then either on cross or in closing (your choice but I think cross may be better), you get her to say that at forty-four feet per second, she had 6.8 seconds to react and stop. Then in the quiet courtroom, look at the clock on the wall and see how long 6.8 seconds is. In a silent courtroom, she had time to go to the store and back in 6.8 seconds. Couple that with the fact that the girls were on the way home from school to change for a prom and that they were running late.

You have totally changed the perception of the facts and the jury's perception of the girls. Imagine what you can do with something more sophisticated.

Computerized video depositions can be used on cross-examination as an effective use by the defense to attack a weak plaintiff's element or to enhance a defense element. The use is through a bar code, which instantly brings up the testimony you want to use. If you use the bar code, the deposition testimony pops up, and the jury sees and hears the damaging testimony. But if you do this, as with any other impeachment, make sure that it does impeach. Go back to the deposition and ask yourself the question, "Do I really have her with this question and answer?"

Another extremely effective use of technology, which is going to get expensive, is the accident reconstruction video.

Rather than have your expert tell the jury how the accident happened, have the expert tell them and show them. With this type of demonstration, you can show how the accident happened the way you want to show it. You can have the jury remember it because they have seen the accident occur. Now switch sides. When faced with a video from the other side, the first thing to do is regain your composure and then start looking at the factual underpinnings. If you can create a doubt about whether all the expert's assumptions are correct, then you can attack the video. Remember, you are dealing not only with your own imagination but also the imagination of the jury. In short, technology's boundaries are only as limited as your imagination will permit it to be. So create and entertain without popcorn in the courtroom.

Adapt technology to the present generation. If you haven't seen the popular "Tasty" videos on Facebook or on YouTube, go watch them. The "Tasty Approach" is how the current generation receives their information. They want as much information as possible, and they want it delivered in an efficient, aesthetically appealing way. In the 1970s, Happy Homemaker shows delivered long, tedious cooking tutorials to the housewives of America. Today, the men and women who cook at home require something much briefer. Tasty delivers recipes to them in an exciting and motivating package.

If you can use technology to break down your trial concepts into small sound bites, easily digestible by the human brain, you will have made huge strides with a present-day jury. Picture it this way. If today's jury had the choice to either watch a one-hour cooking show or could see the entire show in less than a minute (and then move on with their busy lives), which would they pick? Exactly. If you want to impress a jury, don't waste their time. Move forward. Slice the excess off your trial presentation, but retain the important bits of information that they will need to make a decision.

What does this all look like in the symphonic presentation of direct testimony? You start with the witness's script of the facts, add the police investigation with the audio call-in of the accident, bring in the strings with a video reconstruction—the clarinet adds personal tones with the family pictures—and conclude with the percussive photographs of the crumpled cars. You have played one micro out of your total macro.

Appearance and Observation

One of the most important side considerations in a trial is appearance –yours and your client's–and to the extent you can control, your witnesses. You should not look affected–nothing flashy nor anything too tailored. You don't need to stand out. It detracts from the essential elements of your case. After all, the jury is there for the story, not the story-teller. And you don't need the formality of the orchestra, although formal, they are all formally alike. After all, the appearance of the orchestra, like yours, is not important; their harmonic melody, like your symphonic story, is what the jury and the audience are meant to hear.

In terms of appearance, I would suggest another use of video–this time, of the witnesses and the attorneys. Witnesses and attorneys need to see themselves as others see them. Self-examination and critical, positive criticism from others may help heal atonal perception of appearance and mannerisms. Run through a direct examination and see what it looks like. Same thing with an opening statement or closing argument. Ballerinas and concert pianists practice in front of mirrors to see how others see and perceive themselves. So should attorneys and witnesses.

Not only should you be aware that the jurors are watching you, but you should also watch the jurors. What are they telling you on their breaks? Who seems to be the leader in informal talk? What groups hang together? Who is the loner at lunch? If they are in the hall on break, do they read? Talk on the cell phone? This will tell you something about how they are going to go about their deliberations, and you may want to pay attention to some more than others in your presentation of evidence and in your closing arguments without being obvious.

Finally, how should you act during trial? The watchwords are courtesy and respect: courtesy for the opposing counsel, the witnesses, and the court reporter; and respect for the judge. As much as TV may glamorize the tough trial lawyer, juries don't like jerks. Juries tend to prefer fumbling attorneys over rude ones. Again, video yourself and witnesses. How do you come across?

Trial Composition: The Macro Plan

The composition of the trial–the script, if you will–is probably one of the most important facets of a jury trial. Write it all down. One reason that it is so important is because you must constantly deal with Murphy's Law. There should be no surprises that you should have anticipated both from a strategy point and from a mechanical point. By mechanical, I mean the support you bring to the trial of each of the elements, whether it be power point, drawing, or model. It is all the enhancement you provide to the important elements of your case. As I will repeat ad nauseam, if you have dealt with the elements of your case and the mechanics of the trial, you will be able to listen to what is happening around you during the course of the trial and make those adjustments that are necessary based on what you hear.

As I have said before, this is the time to lay out (compose) your trial, your symphony. You will start by laying out the macro plan. Then comes the artistry for each of the micro plans which fit within the macro plan. You have already identified the elements of your causes of action or your defenses from a legal standpoint. When you started, you made sure you covered your bases from a legal standpoint by identifying all possible causes of action and defenses. Now see which of those have been borne out by discovery and discard the ones that just aren't feasible. Staying focused on what really matters helps you stay focused on telling a coherent, tight story. Don't confuse a jury with four different theories of recovery or five defenses. Choose the one that makes sense and go with it.

Once you have eliminated the theories which either don't hold water anymore or confuse the perception of the main element, focus on the elements which form the tone basis for your symphony. We have already seen that you want to enhance the elements which are most important and simply deal with the others. Make certain you cover them. Then identify the witnesses associated with those elements. Who is the most important to use on that element? This leads to a consideration of a planning tool which has been in use for decades—the "order of the witnesses." Whom do we call first? Who is in the middle (and often hidden)? Who is last? This approach is similar to prioritizing highs and lows but not necessarily. For instance, in ordering witnesses, many ascribe to the theory of primacy—that is, the jury will remember most what they heard last. For that reason, if the client is going to get hurt badly on cross-examination, they will not put their client on last. While this theory of witness order must be considered, I think that it is more important to order witnesses based upon their effect on the jury and order the elements of your case, not your witnesses. If a witness will have a powerful emotional impact upon the jury because of his or her demeanor and presentation in presenting one of the elements—but you have not given priority to that element—consider whether to "reorder" the element, not the witness.

In one complex product liability case, the plaintiff put on his expert first to explain in lay terms the complicated engineering terms and concepts which the jury was about to hear in the case. Rather than starting with a chronology of what happened, the testimony gave context to the witnesses who followed and made them more understandable. This element, the expert element, is generally not among the highest in priority; but in this case, it was because without it, the subsequent testimony of the lay witnesses would have been difficult to understand. A guide for the elements to follow was, therefore, created at the outset of the case.

Similarly, in a car wreck case, you may want to put the client on first to lay out the "horrors" of the accident. Again, this is a judgment call of how the emotional elements of your case will play to the jury. I would suggest in ordering your witnesses that you don't put two high-impact, beneficial witnesses together or two witnesses who may hurt the case next to each other, unless your ordering of the elements of the case dictate it. Consider whether to keep the elements together, not the witnesses. Something may get lost with the two high-impact witnesses, and something may get reinforced with the two low-impact witnesses. There are, however, some pretrial aspects of ordering your elements which you may not be able to deal with until the time of trial, such as witness availability. Make any adjustment of the other elements only to accommodate that witness. For your important elements, also consider on what day they will be presented and at what time of the day. The time after lunch and before the afternoon break (does your judge take one) is deadly. This is probably a time when you want to put on one of your less favorable elements.

For a defendant, this map should also be prepared, but be prepared to reorder the elements of the defense based upon what you hear during the plaintiff's case. Has something happened that may cause you to totally reconsider your case and remap your elements? Rethink even your cross-examination in light of what you have heard during the course of the trial?

One more point needs to be discussed in ordering the elements. Obviously, some elements may have more than one witness. If the witness's testimony on an element is repetitious of another witness's testimony, consider whether that witness is necessary. Jurors have commented, "Please tell the lawyers we get it the first time." If the testimony is necessary, make the melody different or introduce with a question, making it clear that this testimony is from a different vantage point.

After the macro map of the case is prepared, then the written microanalysis needs to be done. Microanalysis is prepared for each witness and consists of the script for that witness and the supporting exhibits (the strings, the brass, and the reeds) which you will use with that witness. The amount of supporting exhibits will depend upon whether that witness is for an important element or for an unimportant one. The enhancements for each element and, more particularly, for each witness need to be identified. Identify the witness who will use a particular exhibit and prepare the script for that witness accordingly. When you are identifying the enhancements for each element, make sure you ask, "Why is it being used?" If you can't answer that question, don't use it.

Once both the macro and micro maps of the case have been prepared, you should have a set of "fresh eyes" look at them. You need to walk away from it for a few days and then rereview. A fresh look is necessary to make sure the story is told with the impact you desire.

At this point, some fun begins. When the macros and micros have been prepared, the script and ancillary aids for each witness need to be prepared. When using high-impact exhibits on the screen or monitor to the jury, don't forget to use your display technology (the elmo) with "ordinary" exhibits. If you don't have a laser pen for the witness to use with the document on the screen, get one. It really helps the witness to be able "to point" to the language in the document you want to bring attention to. It also helps point out "where" on the picture the boundary line was drawn.

In your preparation, you will want to deal with the trial notebook. This is your game book (your score if you are the conductor of a symphony), and I don't care how small the case is—prepare it. You should have the case organized with tabs in a notebook for each phase of the trial. Those tabs should begin with the macro and micro sequencing of the presentation of your case or your defense. The other parts of the notebook are the other phases of the trial: voir dire, opening, the micros of your direct and cross, and your closing. By having a road map, it frees you up to think about what is happening rather than worrying about what you are going to do mechanically. Proper mechanical preparation frees your mind to do what you are there for–to listen and think.

One of the most important tabs that you can have in that trial notebook is the cross-examination of each witness. Although you have mapped the micro cross-examination of each witness based upon what you think they will say, be sure, again, to listen to what actually happens during the trial. Be alert to any nuance of difference between the deposition testimony of the witness and the actual testimony. You have already taken the deposition, and you know the points you have scored. If the deposition was taped, you have gone over and over the tapes to watch not only what the witness has said but also how the witness has acted and reacted to questions. Be sure you are ready to impeach with not only what was said but also how it was said. Nonverbal testimony is the music of your story as well and is an area which has not received much attention in the trial of jury cases. You may want to consult your trial consultant or your local symphony conductor. Remember, how it is said is often as important as what is said. You hinge your cross-examination around the answers you have already gotten, and, in your notebook, you have the reference to the page and line in the deposition where that answer was given. You have a copy of that page in your notebook, so you don't have to fumble around searching for it. More dramatically, if you have a video, you have your staff support ready to go straight to the bar code of that answer on the screen so that the jury can hear and see the answer, not just read it.

It used to be that trial preparation only had to cover practicing the direct examination with your client and running through the cross-examination points, together with opening and closing. Now proper preparation involves making sure that you have integrated technology into those phases–and actually using it during preparation to make sure that it works. Fumbling with trying to get documents to appear on the screen is as bad as fumbling through a file looking for that document. If you are in a courtroom with which you are not thoroughly familiar, make sure that you know how to use that court's equipment and, most importantly, make sure yours is compatible with the court's. One final point on this phase of preparation: have a back-up plan if the technology breaks down or doesn't work, even if you have to resort to hard copy. All this lets the jury see that you know what you are doing and builds credibility.

How does the client and, if applicable, the client's onlookers look and act during the trial? This aspect should also have been discussed with them before a videotaped deposition. The wrong clothes and a facial scowl can be devastating to your case. Arrogance is never tolerated. Remember, the jury is constantly unconsciously looking for tonality or atonality and to see who are the good guys and who are the bad guys. The jury is paying close attention to you, your assistants, and your client. If a party is a woman, dress down, and don't wear excessive jewelry. Get rid of pierced body parts. This goes for witnesses too. During the trial, tell "your people" not to react to what is going on. Often you can't see it because they are behind you, but the jury can, and so can the judge. Remind them that on breaks, the jury may see them in the halls or even outside the courtroom. If it is a high-profile case, keep them away from the media and shut down their phone.

Finally, one aspect of trial preparation you may want to consider is a mock trial. If your case potentially has large damages, it really is a "must." With a mock trial, you will get "real juror" reaction to your case, and you will want to make adjustments accordingly. A mock trial will also take you back to the big picture approach and find out what is important and what is only minutiae.

CHAPTER FIVE

INSIDE THE PRACTICE ROOM

ALTHOUGH THE SUBJECT of this chapter could have been included in the chapter on trial preparation, I wanted to highlight it because almost no attention has been given to it in seminars and treatises. That subject is practice. We must emphasize at the outset that if the testimony of a witness is "too practiced," it may come across phony, so a word to the wise: be careful.

The practice room is the center of applied music education. Most undergraduate performance majors at universities practice somewhere between two and six hours per day, while students at conservatories practice even longer hours. This practice does not count for academic credit, nor does a musician receive remuneration for his time spent in practice. Practice time is where the learned concepts are applied to a piece. The pianist takes the concepts that his instructor explained in his lesson and tries them out.

Practice should be repetitive, but it should be "smart" or conscious and built upon self-analysis. Most practice rooms in higher institutions are outfitted with mirrors and sound recording systems so that students can critique, watch, and hear themselves in practice. In practice, students will play a passage using a certain technique or color, and then perhaps they will try it a different way. They will continue to experiment until they have found the perfect tone or color for that particular passage–the tone that works best for them. The important point here for the jury trial analogy is that a music student practices to get it right–not to look good while playing.

Many musicians can talk about the artistic flavor of a piece, that the piece should feel "free" or "weightless," but it is quite another thing to be able to actually play it that way. You have to build up your playing chops or your finger muscle. Practice is inescapable; it is painfully obvious if you haven't put in the necessary amounts of time to perform the piece well. There is absolutely no faking it; without practice, your audience is disgusted with you. You've wasted their time.

Lawyers seem to think that they are immune from the effects of not practicing. This rings especially true for lawyers who have taken trial practice courses. Here's a reference point for you. Those advocacy courses–excellent though they may have been–were your master classes and your private lessons. For you to be able to play a piece or try a jury trial with any level of virtuosity, you must practice. This means that you must take the portions of your jury trial over which you have control (opening, closing, and questions) and rehearse them repetitively. Videotaping yourself is a good idea. Just make sure that you are actually watching and letting others watch the videotape and spending sufficient time in critical evaluation. This concept also applies to the testimony of the witnesses. But a word of warning: don't let it look rehearsed. What you are doing is eliminating or reducing the atonal aspects.

After you have decided that your questions and answers are in line with the appropriate rules, then determine whether you are asking in a way that makes sense for you. Is your demeanor at odds with your appearance? Are you making a hand gesture that seems redundant or overtly artificial? We have seen that one mock trial coach actually carries dumbbells that he places in his students' hands so that they will not wave them about unnecessarily. Ask a friend to watch you ask your questions. Tell him or her to blow a whistle whenever you continue to say one word over and over (especially like the *um*, *like*, or *OK* that is so often overused today). It's important to feel comfortable in front a jury, and that comfortable feeling only comes with practice.

There are plenty of phrases in trial advocacy that can trip you up if you don't know how to use them or even better translate them into everyday jargon. Have you heard, "Let the record reflect that I am directing opposing counsel to what has been premarked for identification as 'Exhibit One?' Forget it. Instead, 'Mr. Jones (the witness), let me show you a diagram of the accident which we've already marked as Exhibit 1' Before you did that, you actually handed opposing counsel a copy of the exhibit.

Hold yourself and your colleagues to a high standard of trial advocacy and preparation. Don't be satisfied to do things the way other attorneys have always done. Most audiences don't want to watch sloppy, ill-rehearsed performances, and most juries will tune out a sloppy, ill-rehearsed attorney. Juries will subconsciously select the most prepared attorney among their available choices. Be that attorney.

Stage fright is a real threat to many attorneys, especially to those who are unaccustomed to jury trials. An excellent book,

The Inner Game of Music, deals specifically with stage fright or performance anxiety from a professional perspective. The book discusses a phenomenon that occurs when a pianist sits down to play. There are two dimensions or pathways of information that the pianist's brain begins to follow as the music begins. First, there is the "interference" or the self-criticism that ensues as the piece begins. The pianist thinks to himself, *Am I playing too loudly? Am I playing too softly? Am I hitting the right notes?* This is a dangerous mind-set to have during a performance. Here is the trouble: the pianist is now focusing on his self-critique, not on the performance.

When a pianist plays a piece, she cannot be focused on whether a baby cried in the audience or whether she flubbed the last passage. She has to focus upon the music. She sees the score in her mind's eye, and she hears the music. She cannot sit and think, *Why did I miss that note three measures ago?* If she does, she will absolutely lose her place in the music. This is the same type of concentration that advocacy requires. Practice is the time for you to hone your skills into a natural style of advocacy. A jury trial is not a rehearsal, and it should never be treated as such. A professional football player once said that during a game, he never heard the crowd. That is concentration.

At this point, it is important for you to distinguish between two practices: actually trying a jury trial and practicing. Practice time is your time to self-reflect and to correct any errors. You may also want to take some time after the jury trial to reflect on what you could have done better. However, you cannot succeed if you second-guess yourself throughout a trial. You cannot focus on you; you have to focus on the jury. This is why it's vital to practice. You must practice—if you want to improve. This is a rare concept in the legal profession but a vital one for those seeking to be true advocacy champions.

PART II

COMPOSITION AND PERFORMANCE

INTRODUCTION

THE DISCUSSION IN this portion of the book will be divided into the five components of the trial, and each is focused on the basic elements which formed your macro plan: voir dire, opening statement, direct examination, cross-examination, and closing argument. Although these five sections will be discussed independently, they should all blend together into a cohesive, harmonious whole through the use of your macro and micro plans. What I mean by that is the voir dire, opening, and closing should be part of your macro plan for the ordering and presentation of the elements, just as those plans for direct and cross are. Each element should be repeated in varying ways in each of those sections. If a part does not fit somewhere into the whole, the harmony is hurt. Under the rules of evidence, that part would be labeled not relevant. Indeed, there is a logical rationale for Rule 401. If it doesn't fit, don't use it because it is not relevant and is atonal to the overall melody.

As you start the preparation of your micro plans, don't lose sight of the macro plan and the overall story. There is an interesting contrapuntal device or musical form known as a fugue. A fugue is a composition in which there is a theme called the subject. The subject is repeated throughout the piece on different pitch levels and in different ways. For a good example of a fugue, listen to track 5. Note the first melody that you hear. After the left hand enters, the subject or theme repeats itself in a higher register. Now it repeats again in a lower register. Without careful concentration, the effect is almost subliminal. Many concertgoers leave the halls humming tunes that their conscious mind never really focused on; this is because the theme was carefully and quietly woven into the music. It should be the same with your piece or trial. Your story, your theme, your words should be the subliminal force that sways the verdict in your favor. Learning to incorporate your theme is a matter of trial and error, but you can improve your ability to do it with practice.

VOIR DIRE

THE TIME HAS arrived. You are ready to start jury selection. If you are from out of town, seek the advice of local counsel. Local counsel is important for the knowledge of local customs, local words and their pronunciation, and, more importantly, your local judge. Knowledge of your local judge, as we have already said, is critical in voir dire. Depending upon what he or she does will dictate whether you get to know your jury. Some judges, for example, do not let lawyers conduct the voir dire. In that situation, you don't know the tone of your jury as well. Does the judge permit backstriking (excusing a juror in later rounds if accepted in all earlier rounds)? Is private questioning out of the presence of other jurors permitted as to what you will be permitted to do, both from a formality-informality standpoint but also from a procedural standpoint? Are jurors selected in sequential order from a list? If there is a list, what information is on it? You may even want to know how juries are empaneled. Are they selected, or do the first panels consist of volunteers from those who have been summoned for jury duty?

Once you have lists of jurors and panels (if there are lists), run them by others in your firm or your local counsel's firm. Do an Internet search on them. You may be surprised by what you find. What is the neighborhood like in which they live? Who are their neighbors? See if anyone knows them. Do any of them have children? If so, what is the feeder school they are zoned to attend? There is a wealth of information you may obtain even before you walk into the first morning of trial.

Next, we need to return to the concept of "tonality." If something is tonal, it is pleasing. If it is atonal, a jury is repulsed by it. In this process of juror selection, we are trying to learn what is tonal or atonal to each individual juror and what may be tonal or atonal to the jury as a whole.

Voir dire is the process of charting a juror's individual tonality to try to determine the tonality of the jury as a whole. If voir dire is performed skillfully, you will be able to determine the spectrum of the jury's tonality–their comfort zone. Once you have found that spectrum, you can think about the statements that you need to make and determine where they fall on the chart we discussed in chapter 1.

To digress a bit here, you need to understand that determining tonality is a process that only begins with voir dire. It continues throughout the trial. Too often, legal assistants just shuffle papers and carry coffee. Use them, however, to casually watch the jury throughout the trial and during breaks. If your assistant sees a juror flinch or smirk, make sure she records that body language. This procedure will help you develop and refine your juror tonality spectrum long after voir dire is finished. Be careful. Don't be obvious; jurors don't like to be studied.

Tuning a jury is similar to tuning a symphony orchestra. Before the conductor takes his introductory bow, before his baton lifts, and before the magic that is music occurs, a lone figure grasping a violin steps out onto the stage. His or her job is largely ceremonial, but the process is important. He or she plays one note. In reality, an impatient oboe overtakes his or her position and plays the note for her or his for the first time. A single, strident "A" vibrates through the hall, and soon after, the strings echo sweeter, softer "As."

The musicians are becoming one. They are "getting in tune," listening, making sure that every instrument is on the same page, that they are harmonious. Make no mistake; they tuned before they sat down on stage. Now a greater miracle has to occur–they have to be in tune, together. They listen to each other. They must be in tune with each other, and for this job, the concertmaster is important. In a jury trial, you are concertmaster. Through your selection process, you are actually tuning the jury because you are looking for that group of twelve that are in tune, as a whole, with your performance. Unlike a symphony, the jurors do not necessarily know that they are in tune with each other. That is your job to determine.

Now that I have discussed what you want, let's discuss how you want to do it. You are looking for that atonal juror–one that is not in tune with your melody.

Thus, the aim of voir dire is not only to be in tune with the jury but also to see if the jurors are in tune with each other. At this point, it's safe to assume that the lawyer is in tune with himself. The question then becomes, is he in tune with the jury? And then is the jury in tune with each other? In addition to its original purpose of filtering through a juror's biases, voir dire should be a conversation in which the lawyer gets to know the individual whom he wants in tune with his or her case.

If the trial revolves around a particular act or practice, find out if any juror is familiar with the act or practice, particularly if it is part of her work. If the juror has that familiarity, stop and ask the judge if you can continue the voir dire out of the presence of the other jurors. If that juror's practice is at odds with the practice you are asking the jurors to accept, that juror is atonal, and you want to excuse him. In addition, if you ask the juror his knowledge of the act or practice in front of the others, you risk infecting them with the atonality of that juror, and they may inadvertently become atonal.

Don't ask the question which is going to get a "yes" or "no" answer unless you are simply trying to get the juror to commit to some principal, such as whether they can award large damages. The most important point I can make as a suggestion for voir dire is to get the jurors talking. If your trial judge, in his or her initial discussion with the jurors, does not explain that in the voir dire phase the lawyers are not trying to pry into your private lives, then do it yourself. Explain you are just trying to find out about your life experiences to see if you will identify with one side or the other. You have got to get them talking. You have got to see if they are in tune with you. You have got to listen! What is that juror telling you, and what is she not telling you?

You are trying to find out how the juror ticks, how he or she thinks. Are they in tune with and sympathetic to the theme you are conveying? For this process in which you are trying to predict human decisions based upon human behavior, you need to consider engaging a jury consultant. We know a consultant is not within the budget for a small case, but for a case which could have a potentially large price tag, it is well worth the money. Not only is it worth it for jury selection but also for advice during the trial.

You should not be the talker. It is your job to get the juror to answer in whole sentences and thoughts. After all, you need to find out how they think. As you engage a juror, watch the reaction of other jurors. Are they nodding? Although there is no list of questions to ask prospective jurors, there are certain topics which you probably need to cover. If you represent the plaintiff and are seeking a large award, you need to get their reaction to the possibility of a large damage award. Although the initial response to these questions may be "Yes" or "No," follow up with "Why?" or "Why not?" Would you be willing to vote for a large amount? Do you believe in damages for pain and suffering? Do you believe in lawsuits? Do you have any religious beliefs that would keep you from bringing back a verdict for the plaintiff? For a large amount? The old standard "bumper sticker" question is not a bad one but make sure you understand what the bumper sticker is saying about them. If you don't recognize a sticker that they have told you about, ask them what it is for or why they have put it on their car. They will talk, and in doing that, you will learn about them. If you ask them what magazines they read, ask them why. Although society now does not take a likin' to stereotyping, we are afraid, as I have said, that this is exactly what you are doing. It is what you have to do to make the decision on keeping a juror or not.

Another thing you are trying to find out in this process is if there is a leader. Is this juror a bass drum or a tinkling bell? I have heard jury consultants say, and I agree, that whether you are a plaintiff or a defendant, you don't want a leader because you can't take the risk on which way he or she may lead. How do you find a leader? Well, have they formed any organizations, or do they belong to any? What type? What does it do? This may also tell you if they are atonal. Are they active in community affairs? What do they do? Do they belong to any organizations? Which? What do they do? Have they been an officer? Been on the board? What organizations do they contribute to? And the list goes on and on. Use your imagination. Then make your decision. Is this person in tune with my theme?

Above all, listen to the answer. What is this person telling me about how he or she will decide this case? Have I asked enough questions to really find out everything I need to know? This rule applies throughout the trial, whether it is a juror, a witness, or even the judge. An example of an attorney not listening to the question of a prospective juror involved a very serious automobile accident which later resulted in a $15 million jury verdict. During that jury selection, a juror was asked whether she possessed a valid driver's license, a common question, to which she responded, "No." The attorney did not follow up and ask, "Why don't you have a license?" Later, consultation with the prospective juror disclosed that the reason she did not have a valid driver's license was because she was legally blind. She was very young and did not look blind. In that same case, jurors were asked if they knew the plaintiff, and one prospective juror responded that she had babysat for his children when she was younger. The lawyer stopped there and did not ask when the last time the juror had seen the plaintiff. If asked, she would have said that she was in the emergency room the night he was brought in from the accident.

You are now about to wind up your selection process, and you are down to your last peremptory challenge. Make sure at this point you have another challenge. If you are in a jurisdiction where challenges are announced rather than passed to the judge on a slip and you think you have one more challenge but you don't and announce a challenge, you have just totally alienated that juror whom you tried to excuse. Next, if you have only one more challenge, try to eyeball the juror who will be next in the jury box if you excuse a juror. If jurors are wearing badges with numbers, this is fairly easy to do; and looking at the background information on your jury list, you get some idea whether the replacement is better than the one you want to excuse.

Your jury is selected and sworn. It is now time to start to play the symphony. But you are not yet quite through with voir dire. It is now time to reflect on who is left in the jury box. What is the tone or tune of those individuals? Do they have something in common with each other? Do they have something in common with your tone? Take the time, if you have it, to see if there are any changes to be made to the macro plan.

THE OPENING STATEMENT

INTERESTINGLY, AS IN most areas of the trial, there is no "right" way to make an opening statement, but there are plenty of wrong ways. First, make sure that you are not atonal. Be yourself and don't be condescending or don't instruct the jury. Talk with them. Video yourself making your opening statement and critique it. Arrange the opening around the elements and the theme which you have prepared in your macro plan. When an audience comes to hear a symphony orchestra play a piece, they probably have heard it before and want to see how this orchestra and conductor will play it. Your jury, however, has never heard your masterpiece before, so you need not only to tell them the story and its elements but also familiarize them with the players, the witnesses, the good, and the bad. If you haven't done it in voir dire, you need to bring out some of the warts in your case to start dealing with them. You want to deal with them, even if they are bad facts or unusual physical traits of a witness.

It has also been stated by many courts that opening statements are merely to inform the trial judge and jury, in a general way, of the nature of the case and to outline, generally, the facts each party intends to prove. But this rule does not mean that you must be mechanical in your opening. A word of caution: know what your trial judge will permit. How close can you get to actual argument in your opening? However you do it, you need to start using your element lingo and emphasizing the important elements you have identified in your macro plan. Keep the lawyer lingo out, such as "We expect to prove . . ." Well, who else is going to prove it? Tell the story. If you stick to facts, you can't be called down for trying to argue the case—yet. People love to listen to a good storyteller. When preparing for your opening statement, be aware that exhibits may not be used in the opening statement without the agreement of all parties and permission of the court. The reason for this rule is that the exhibits are not yet in evidence and may not be shown to the jury. This is not to say that you can't draw on an easel to portray what you are saying, such as drawing the intersection and showing how the accident happened. Remember, since it is not an exhibit, the other side can use it and even draw on it to show how they say the accident happened. A word of caution: a juror might find that this is rude.

Now to the presentation of the opening itself. If you can do it without notes, do it without notes. If you must use notes, do it in bullet forms with the bullets being the main topics you want to cover. One opening was done ingeniously with small boards that counsel set up along the front of the jury box so it would not look like she was using notes. We don't know whether the jury saw the boards she used, but it was a creative way to do an opening.

In your opening, you are the jury's friend; and as their friend, you are about to tell them a story. You are explaining what this case is about. Forget the lawyer jargon, such as, "Ladies and gentlemen, the plaintiff will prove to you in this case that the defendant is responsible for this motor vehicle accident, and you should return a verdict for him or her." What's a plaintiff? What's a motor vehicle accident? What's going on? Rather, start out by introducing your case, such as, "My client, Peggy Jones, was driving down Broad Street one afternoon, and the defendant, Johnny Culprit, ran a stop sign and hit her in the driver door." Now the jury knows there are two drivers, that your client is the good guy, and the bad guy who caused the accident is the defendant. Then you can go into background, other circumstances of the accident, damages, etc., but you have told them up front what the case is about, who the main actors are, and you have dealt heavily on your main elements. If, as a plaintiff, your strong elements are the cause of the accident and damages, emphasize them. If, as a defendant, your strong element is a preexisting condition, emphasize that. Start using and keep using the names of the elements of your cause of action and your theme. They will be used again in direct and cross, in closing, and most importantly, in the judge's charge.

Are there any other helpful hints with respect to openings? Probably, but they may depend on the facts of each case. Generally, I wouldn't advise using the terms *plaintiff* and *defendant*. Who are they? What are their names? Also, if you have not already done it in voir dire, you may want to deal with some of your problems here. If your client has written some bad memos or said some stupid things, admit that up front. Don't let the jury discover on its own that your client is a jerk. Be sure to tell the client you are going to do this. They will take ownership of an issue which they have discovered. A jury does not like a lawyer who tries to "finesse" an issue.

If liability is admitted, tell them that your client is responsible for the accident and that their only role is to figure out what the reasonable damages are. You start to add credibility with this approach. If you have weaknesses, deal with them. Know the old phrase, "If you're explaining, you're losing." You have to explain why your client did what he did, and that lets you start to tell your story. As one commentator used to say, "And that is the rest of the story." With a weakness, explain it and then fit it into the whole theory of your case. If there is going to be graphic evidence, warn them of that too. In short, don't let them learn of bad stuff during the trial.

Finally, be brief. If your opening is too long, the jury may start out confused. If your case is simple, keep the opening simple. If the case is complicated, uncomplicate it. Remember, keep to the big picture.

DIRECT EXAMINATION

DIRECT EXAMINATION SHOULD be one of the most boring parts of the trial for the lawyer because it is the witness that the jury should hear.

You have prepared the macro plan of your elements. Now let's see what a micro plan for a witness looks like by taking a hypothetical macro plan for the plaintiff in a car wreck case. She is presenting not only the facts of the accident but also more importantly the severity of the injury. You are, therefore, starting the preparation of her micro plan with two Schenkerian notes upon which you will build. I suggest you start with the accident note and finish with the damage note.

At this point, start to build the presentation, not just her testimony. Her testimony is the building blocks. With her presentation, you start to add the symphony of the mortar, the exhibits, the visual aids, the audio aids (such as the actual reporting of the police call-in), the photographs–all those things which will let the jury see and hear the element which is the crash. The accident starts with what she was doing and where she was going when she went to her car. It also covers why any passenger may have been with her. Have her take the jury step by step with what she did before the accident–you are creating drama. Show a video of what she saw. Then if you can do it, use the clock. By this, I mean if you can translate distance and speed into time to show reaction time, it may work for you. By this, I mean if the distance and speed show that the defendant had 4.2 seconds to react, show it, but do it quietly with a courtroom second hand (if there is one). Elapsed time of 4.2 seconds in a quiet courtroom is an eternity. After going through this experience, have her graphically describe the impact. Then amplify on your note with a picture of the wrecked vehicles and how much damage resulted to her car. Then more pictures of the huge truck. Now take her through the trip to the emergency room and subsequent treatment. Make your story come alive.

Finally, end her testimony with "the day in the life of" using five or six (no more) significant photos of how she used to be able to play with her grandchildren, including playing with them but being unable to pick them up. Once the micro plan has been prepared, run through it several times, not only to practice it but also to see how it looks and sounds. In preparing her testimony, make sure that it is kept conventional.

If we were going to assign a musical form to direct examination, it would be "concerto." A concerto is a showpiece composition, in which an instrumental soloist is accompanied by an orchestra. For the sake of our analogy, the lawyer is the orchestra, and the client is the soloist. Just because all eyes are on the witness does not mean that you do not have a part to play. You play a supportive, complementary role to your witness by setting them up with the most effective questions and by giving them the impetus and direction of the story. Listen to track 6, and using your imagination, see yourself as the conductor of the orchestra and the piano as the client. You begin the process with a single, simple question. Your questions continue to delve into the story, giving the witness the ability to break free, to feel comfortable telling the jury her version of the event. You and the witness continue to play off each other, but you are constantly a bit "under" the witness in volume, so to speak. You defer to the witness, but you support her with appropriate questions that remind her of her main points. You give her a chance in the spotlight, while your questions add to her credibility and tonality with the jury. Don't be afraid to use emphasis questions, such as "Do you mean to say . . .?" or "Did you really just say that . . . ?"

Once the testimony has been scripted, run through it as many times as it takes the witness to be comfortable with what she is doing. For some witnesses, this may be one or two times. For others, it may be more, but don't keep rehearsing to the point that the witness becomes frustrated or that it looks rehearsed. You don't want fresh, exciting testimony to become atonal so that it begins to sound memorized and scripted.

Although we try not to lay down rules in this work, there is one rule on direct examination that must be followed. That rule is that he or she who prepares the witness puts the witness on the stand. Why? Well, let me give you an example of why. In a complex commercial case, the main witness for the defense in a securities case was the one who was going to tell the whole story of why the commercial paper of a company had been rated prime. This witness had been subjected to cross-examination after cross-examination in depositions and by the Securities and Exchange Commission. But now, in the trial, he was going to tell the story his way. He was extremely well prepared for his direct examination and taken through it several times but not by the lawyer who was putting him on the stand. The lawyer who would conduct the examination did watch it and was satisfied. The witness was great and was the key to the defense. Unfortunately, the dialect and cadence of the person who prepared the witness was totally different from that of the person who put him on the stand. When the witness took the stand, he got out his name, address, and employer just fine. But it was totally downhill from there, including that fact that he did not even recognize some of the documents in the company file. The trial adjourned and was settled. The witness had simply not had a chance to become comfortable with the persona, dialect, and cadence of the person who put him on the stand. So he who prepares the witness must put him on the stand.

The next suggestion is not a rule in preparing the script but involves the use of common sense. Let the witness tell the story. Don't tell it with your questions. The jury is present to hear the witness, not some lawyer who was not even there. Make sure that the wittiness is a storyteller, not a teacher or actor but someone who relates–or tells or shares. And listen to the answer. Make sure that it was the one you were expecting. If not, go back over it to pick up on things which may have been inadvertently left out.

Also, I have often heard lawyers in preparing a witness tell the witness to look at the jury when they testify. This is good advice unless it looks contrived. If the lawyer is at the lectern for the questioning and the witness has to turn to look at the jury after every question, it looks phony. This approach will work if the judge permits you to conduct the examination of the witness from the end of the jury box where the witness has to look across the jury to the questioner. But be careful with what you take to the end of the jury box to assist you. If you can see it, the jury might be able to see it too.

Now what do you do with something which may be damaging in the testimony? Some say wait for cross-examination because if you bring it out on direct, you are "vouching" for bad testimony. I question that. If the testimony is bad, it is bad.

Deal with it. It is better to bring bad testimony out on direct with your explanation rather than get killed with it on cross and then have to "explain" it on redirect. How you deal with it is important. Trying to hide it is often worse than simply acknowledging it and moving forward. If you wait for that testimony on cross, it may look like you are trying to hide it, giving the other side what is called an a-hah. If you wait for it to come out on cross, you likely will lose credibility with the jury. You can acknowledge that the testimony is bad without conceding your case by dealing with it and giving it your "best look," not the other side's "worst look." When all else fails, concede the point and offer to stipulate.

Finally, after the direct and cross, consider carefully whether you need to conduct a redirect examination. If you do conduct that redirect, it will open your witness up to recross. Also, remember that on redirect, unlike cross, you are confined to the scope of the cross.

Once you have scripted all the direct examination micro plans, go back in your mind and make sure your macro plan still works. Is there something about the rehearsals that causes you to rethink your sequence of your elements? I suggest that you video your rehearsals so that you can show your client what she or he looks like testifying and see what the jury will see. It will also help you rethink your macro and micro plans. Also, video the person who is putting the witness on the stand to see if there are any negatives in the tone of voice, mannerism, or appearance.

CROSS-EXAMINATION

IN APPROACHING CROSS-EXAMINATION, I will again use our new friend, Heinrich Schenker. In planning the direct examination, I used his technique to plan our major and minor elements, and I proceeded somewhat methodically. You might think that I do not have that luxury in cross-examination, but I do. In cross, I have the ability to simply disregard the elements where the other side is not vulnerable and focus on the ones that are. Let me emphasize here: do not be tempted to cross-examine on all the elements or a myriad of details presented by the case. *My blunt advice for cross-examination is to be brief! Pick your strong points (his or her weak points) and sit down.* Otherwise, the points will be lost in a two-hour rambling examination, which is really not a cross-examination. And when you have made them, make it look like you have made them.

A symphony analogy is particularly appropriate here. In a Yale University composition class, the students were asked to compose using only four notes. One student returned after the assignment and complained that no piece could possibly be composed with four notes; it was not enough. It was too simple. The professor responded, "What about ᵗᵗₜ (da-da-da-dum)?" as in the opening of Beethoven's "Fifth Symphony." If Beethoven, the plodding composer, could start a symphony with only four notes, you can conduct a cross-examination with only five questions, carefully crafted.

Let me digress to make another point about brevity. If you choose to cross-examine your opponent's strong element, you will detract from your cross-examination of the witness on *your* strong point. You may actually detract from your total cross-examination either by losing control of the witness or by becoming atonal with the witness and actually alienating the jury. An example is appropriate. In a personal injury case, the defendant had admitted negligence (not liability because causation was reserved), and the plaintiff had called two witnesses to testify on the plaintiff's damages–her mother and her best friend. Their testimony had not really hurt the defendant because they were expected to testify to what a good person the plaintiff was and to some of the things that she used to be able to do. Rather than the attorney stating he had no questions of those nice people whose testimony had not been very emotional or exaggerated, defense counsel attacked them. This almost resulted in the loss with the jury of some of the points gained by admitting negligence in the case. If any point was to be made, it was with the plaintiff's doctor, not lay witnesses.

When you conduct your cross-examination, don't be so infatuated with your brilliance that you forget to listen to what the witness is saying. Ask yourself, "What did the witness just say?" Is there anything on direct he didn't say? If not, why not? Did he say something different from the way he said it in deposition? Listen and see if you can understand.

And don't hurry your cross-examination. Slow down and let the jury follow and understand you. Don't rush past the important points you make in your cross-examination. Let them sink in on the jury. Let the jury understand that they are important. You may be so excited to make your point that you forget who is supposed to be excited–you or the jury. Answer: the jury. You figured this point out before trial, and that's when you should get excited–about using what you have found. And when you do it, savor the moment.

One perfect example occurred in a case involving the construction of an apartment complex. The contractor sued the shingle supplier, contending that the shingles he bought for the complex leaked. The supplier's expert had tested one of the shingles from the job in every way possible and could not make them leak. Case over? Let's see. The lab director who oversaw the testing testified in detail about the various tests used, which had resulted in no leaking. In starting the cross, counsel knew in advance that the expert had tested the wrong shingle because his contractor-client had bought 99 percent of the shingles for the job at a special price before construction even began, and the tested shingle had been manufactured after the job was almost finished. The client had run out of the original purchase and had to buy some extras to finish the job. The one tested by the expert was not part of the original shipment; it was one of the extras. The way that the contractor knew all this was because the date of manufacture of the shingle was on it, and the test report showed that date. When counsel excitedly began his cross-examination, he went back over the test the expert had performed. But then he asked very quietly, "And after all these tests, you couldn't make that shingle leak?" He proudly announced that he could not. There was a pause, and the attorney then asked, "Did you know you tested the wrong shingle?" He, of course, said no. When showed the purchase invoice and its date, he responded, "Oh no!" The cross-examination stopped there. Case over.

Another suggestion for cross-examination is a gutsy one. If there are multiple defendants in a case and if the witness has not touched your client on direct examination, don't be afraid to say in front of the jury that your client has no questions of this witness. (Be sure to explain why in your closing, but right now, you have silently said this witness didn't hurt me.)

Sometimes on cross, you really won't know the answer to an important question that arises because of developments during the trial. Most lawyers will tell you not to ask a question when you don't know the answer. I disagree, but approach this type of question cautiously. You may want to try this technique. You start with innocuous questions. In a car accident, it might be "What were you doing before the accident? Looking at billboards? Listening to the radio? Thinking about the last meeting you attended? Talking on the cell phone? Or just talking to the passenger?" If you get enough good stuff, you can then ask, "So you weren't really paying attention?" You don't care what the answer to this question is because if it is "No, I wasn't." You have a great answer. If it was "Yes, I was," the witness is lying, and you have made your point. Be sure to remind the jury of this in closing.

Finally, as with direct examination, please video your cross-examination during rehearsal of it. Working with a witness in rehearsal will not only hone your skills; it will also let you see if you have become atonal in the cross-examination. Have you become aggressively offensive, or are you still Columbo?

So what have you accomplished in our cross-examination of the witness? If you are the defendant, we have given an advance view of the strong elements in our case. If you are the plaintiff, you have reinforced the strong elements of our case. But above all, be brief. It is easier for the jury to be impressed by and remember one or two points rather than ten.

CLOSING ARGUMENT

BEFORE DISCUSSING THE content of the closing, let me make one brief comment on the conduct of counsel during closing. Not only is the subject of the conduct of counsel important in discussing closing, it is also important in discussing it in the context of the entire trial, whether it be a jury trial or a bench trial. Indeed, it is fair to say that the subject of the conduct of counsel is a fair topic for further discussion. This subject has even been the rationale for the creation by Justice Warren Berger of the American Inns of Court, an institution created to instill civility in the conduct of a trial lawyer.

Touching briefly on the subject, however, it is an area where there is a dearth of published court opinions which discuss the conduct of counsel, except perhaps in those proceedings which are so contemptuous as to warrant discipline. But there are boundaries which I will not cover here other than to say that offensive conduct is not only offensive to the system; it is also offensive to the jury. The last thing you want a jury to see is a rude, arrogant, contentious lawyer. It will destroy an otherwise good case. So watch how you are perceived by the jury.

Let me start a discussion of the closing argument with a specific point through an analogy. In growing up as children, we were taught to savor our food. That often meant "saving the best for last." If you do that in a jury trial by saving the best argument for your closing argument, you have lost the case. By that time, the jury will have formed a general opinion of the case. Your closing is to reinforce that opinion, not inject something new. I once observed a medical malpractice case where an important part of that case was a telephone call from the emergency room doctor to the personal doctor of the plaintiff. That call was memorialized in a very cryptic file note which contained abbreviations which, it turned out, were not the words normally associated with those abbreviations. Plaintiff's counsel, however, did not provide the translation until his closing. It is still a mystery why he didn't provide it with the witness. He lost the case.

In preparing for your closing, review what actually happened in the case and whether it differs from or changes your macro plan. If there hasn't been some surprise during the trial, then you did not try your case on planet earth. Deal with those surprises in your closing as well as your planned closing. Again, practice that closing! In a case which lasted eighty-six trial days, each counsel was allotted ninety minutes to close. That sounds like a long time, but covering eighty-six days of trial in ninety minutes was no mean feat. That closing was rehearsed, refined, and "trained" five times before it was actually given.

The preparation of your closing will still focus, as it has during the trial, on those Schenkerian elements which are important to your case. Those elements in your closing, however, will now coincide with the elements on which the judge will instruct the jury in his charge, as this continuum is very important. Using some of the same words in your closing, which will appear in the charge, will give credibility to your case—both your presentation of them during the trial and in your discussion of them in your closing. Give them the same emphasis in our closing you gave them in your trial.

Your closing, however, depends not only upon your prioritization of the elements but also on what has gone right and what has gone wrong with them during the trial. Although it will be carefully prepared, you should prepare for your closing argument with the foreknowledge that you should not read it to the jury. Be able to visualize the five or six main points of your closing, and you should be able to deliver an extemporaneous closing. You can even jot them down. Practice it in front of others. It will get you used to delivering it to the jury. Your closing argument must sound like you mean it, not be simply a memorized speech.

Although you should argue positively and forcefully in your closing, conceding a losing point can be just as effective. For example, the following has been used effectively. The case is a car accident, and there is admitted negligence. Rather than contest every dollar that the plaintiff is asking for, concede that certain expenses incurred by the plaintiff are reasonable, "and we don't contest those expenses. The plaintiff should be awarded them." This gives you credibility with the jury.

Next, don't get locked into your argument just because that is what you rehearsed. Again, the rule. Listen to what the other side is saying. But do rehearse it and video it. Watch yourself critically. Are you becoming atonal, patronizing, or boring? Don't be too proud to get constructive criticism. On a procedural note, be sure to clear the amount of time you have for closing with the court. First, a reasonable amount of time to close is necessary. For the court to allow thirty minutes for a closing instead of forty-five is, however, not abuse.

Finally, although the plaintiff has the right to open and close, don't forget that if defense counsel does not conduct a closing argument on a particular point, plaintiff's counsel may not respond. So watch yourself.

Finally, as I said above–and it bears repeating–use the judge's charge in your closing. In order to assist counsel in making the closing argument, the trial judge should rule upon requests to charge prior to the making of the closing argument. Some courts have held that counsel may not include statements about the law in the closing argument. I believe that is incorrect and that this argument should be permitted. If the trial judge has given you a copy of the charge, you should be able to read from it in closing arguments and state that the language is from the charge the judge will give shortly. But make sure you can. It is very effective to weave together the judge's words in the charge with the testimony of your witnesses on those elements which are your strength.

CODA

LAWYER AND COMPOSERS have a lot in common, but perhaps their closest tie is that they are both employed in the art of making something out of nothing. Have you ever really listened to Beethoven's "Fifth Symphony," particularly the clichéd first movement? (Listen to track 7.) The piece is built upon a simple rhythm, and yet our minds perceive the piece to be so complicated. Composers refer to their ability to create a sophisticated, nuanced piece out of tiny musical ideas as "economy of material." This is ultimately your task. You may have something as simple as a car wreck, but if you are an artist, that car wreck case can become something magnificent. Now in your next jury trial, "Good luck and listen."

TRACKS

1. Schenkerian Analysis: Foreground, Foreground Reduction, Middle Ground, Background (Ursatz)
2. Beethoven, Ludwig van: Symphony no. 7, Movement 2
3. Mozart, Wolfgang Amadeus: Piano Sonata in B-flat Major, K. 333, Movement 1
4. Crumb, George: "Black Angels," Movement 1, "Departure"
5. Bach, Johann Sebastian: Fugue no. 12 in F Minor, WTC II, BWV 881
6. Prokofiev, Sergei: Piano Concerto no. 3, Movement 1
7. Beethoven, Ludwig van: Symphony no. 5, Movement 1

ABOUT THE AUTHOR

NEIL THOMAS

THE AUTHOR IS a retired trial judge with twenty years of experience on the civil bench and over twenty-five years of experience as a trial attorney. As a trial judge, he presided over two hundred jury trials. As a trial attorney, he participated in the defense of what was at that time the longest jury trial in the Sixth Federal Judicial Circuit. His education was at the University of North Carolina and the University of Michigan Law School. He has both lectured and taught on the subjects of jury selection, evidence, and trial strategy. Thomas blends his trial experience from his practice in New York and then Chattanooga with his years on the state court bench where he presided over trials involving complex contract disputes, medical malpractice, and products liability. His professional involvement has included service on the governing body of the Litigation Section of the American Bar Association and in the House of Delegates of the Tennessee Bar Association. He founded the Litigation Section of the Tennessee Bar Association. He is a fellow of the American, Tennessee, and Chattanooga Bar Foundations and is a member of the bar of the United State Supreme Court. His community service includes president of the Chattanooga Chamber of Commerce, the Chattanooga Rotary Club, the Brock-Cooper American Inns of Court, the Tennessee Safety Council, Junior Achievement; and friends of both Chickamauga National Military Park and Moccasin Bend Park and the Salvation Army. He has published and taught extensively in the legal field. His publications and presentations are as follows:

Empirical Articles in Peer Review Journals

Benton, T. R, McDonnell, S., Thomas, N., Ross, D. F., and Honerkamp, N. (2006). On the admissibility of expert testimony on eyewitness identification: A legal and scientific evaluation. *Tennessee Journal of Law and Policy,* 3, 392–452.

Rapus-Benton, Ross, D. F., McDonnell, S., Thomas, N., and Bradshaw, M. (2006). Eyewitness Memory is Still Not Common Sense: Comparing Jurors Judges and Law Enforcement to Eyewitness Experts. *Applied Cognitive Psychology,* 20, 115–129.

Bradshaw, G. S., Ross, D. F., Bradshaw, E., Headrick, B. and Thomas, N. (2005). Fostering Juror Comfort: Effects of an Orientation Videotape. *Law and Human Behavior,* 29, 4, 457–469.

Book Chapters

Benton, T., McDonnell, S., Ross, D. F., Thomas, N. and Bradshaw, E. (2007). Has eyewitness testimony penetrated the American legal system? A synthesis of case history, juror knowledge, and expert testimony. Chapter in Lindsay, R. C. L., Ross, D., Read, D., and Toglia, M. (Eds). *Handbook of Eyewitness Psychology: Volume 1 Memory for People.* Lawrence Erlbaum Publishing, Mahwah, NJ.

Invited Presentations, Continuing Legal Education Training Seminars

Ross, D. F. and Thomas, N. (2010). Science in the Courtroom, American Inns of Court.

Ross, D. F. and Thomas, N. (2010). Understanding the factors defined in Daubert. Chattanooga Bar Association, Continuing Legal Education Seminar.

Ross, D. F. and Thomas, N. (2001). On the Psychology of Jury Selection and Behavior. Chattanooga Bar Association, Continuing Legal Education Seminar.

Ross, D. F. and Thomas, N. (2004). Teaching Judges about Science. Invited address given at the Tennessee Judicial Conference, Memphis TN.

Ross, D. F. and Thomas, N. (2004). Detecting Deception: Is it possible? Invited address given to the Nashville Bar Association, Nashville, TN.

Ross, D. F. and Thomas, N. (2003). Psychology and View from the Bench. Invited address given to the Nashville Bar Association, Nashville, TN.

Ross, D. F. and Thomas, W. Neil (2001). On the Psychology of Jury Selection and Jury Behavior. Invited address and CLE seminar given to the Chattanooga Bar Association.

Conference Presentations: (Peer Reviewed)

Bradshaw, B., Ross, D. F., Dunlap, E., and Thomas, N. (2003). "Further exploration into the effects of an orientation videotape on juror knowledge and comfort." Paper presented at the meeting of the American Psychology and Law Society, Edinburgh, Scotland.

Dunlap, E., Ross, D.F., Bradshaw, B., Nell, R., and Thomas, N. (2003). "Is eyewitness testimony commonsense to jurors?" Paper presented at the meeting of the American Psychology and Law Society, Edinburgh, Scotland.